# A New Horizon of Music Therapy



Including subtle and scholarly exploration of the character of the Indian Ragas, selection of Scale and Dose of Music at the time of Therapy

Basumitra Majumder

Made with ❤ on the Notion Press Platform

www.notionpress.com

To my Parents,
Who embeded aesthetic & musical sense
in my mind and ears.

# Contents

# Author's Preface

I am pleased to introduce a new chapter of Music Therapy to the well-being of people.

In this book, I have discussed the process and method of curing diseases through listening to the tune of music or any rhythm, etc., as suggested by Astrology.

Astrology believes that any disease is a cause of planetary weakness; likewise, every swar of Indian music is influenced by any planet. That is why each raga conveys different sentiments and emotions.

Therefore, after detecting the disease, if we apply the raga or melody of that planet-affected swar to alleviate that planet, the patient can get relief from the disease as soon as the planetary weakness is removed. Based on this concept, we have prepared this book.

There are many other books on music therapy. But our book is written from an entirely new perspective. This book will benefit human society.

# Why is this Book for

When I was a student of Astrology, my teacher respectable Sukracharya (Jitendra Bhushan Palit), told me that an astrologer could only guide a person. He advised, "People will come to you as stricken with problems, and you only lead them in that disorienting situation. But don't try to sell the gemstone unnecessarily."

So, after completing my studies, I would started my work as Astrology-practitioner. People come to me with their problems, and I used to advise them as per my knowledge.

At that time, one thing captured my thought. With rising commodity prices, how can a person buy a precious stone as an astrologer prescribes? Can we get another method to save on expenditure?

That was the end of the last century or the beginning of this century; I read a short chapter on the Pythagorean Astrological concept of Music. Then I tried to apply that concept to Indian Music. But there is some difference between both musical systems. So, I tried to Indianise that approach. That was a little article published in an Astrological Magazine at that time.

After that, I got some hands-on opportunities to apply my theories. Then, after a few experiments, I could express my thought and researched broadly to other practitioners. Those reflections and inspirations made me busy with this research.

One day a client came to me with his problems. After listening to his situation when I was preparing his birth chart for prediction, he suddenly said, 'Sir, look here, my leg has vanished from my knee.' His mother, about eighty years old, wept and said, 'Please do something to cure my son. I went to the doctor, who prescribed some medicine, but my son did not take that properly. He compares those medicines with the internet and takes as he desires.' And after some conversation, I discovered that the client was a player of *Tabla* (a pair of drums), and he can remember a few *Bols* (onomatopoeia) like *Trital, Jhaptal, Teora, Dadra, Kaharba* etc.

My spiritual guide said, "*Do Kirtan, and the mind will be purified.*" So, by remembering his words, I advised my client to recite those *Bols* repeatedly throughout the day in his leisure time. Then, after six or more months, when I had almost forgotten him, he came to me and said he was free from all problems. He was embarrassed by remembering his 'leg-vanished' utters.

Another client came to me with her mother and aunt. The girl was about twenty or twenty-two. Her mother asked about her marriage. Suddenly the girl shouted, 'Look, look! So many black insects are emerging from my body and capturing my hand and body. Can't you see those insects?' I refuged to lie, 'Yes, yes. But just now, they have gone.' She said, 'Yes sir, all are gone inside my body. You looked at them, but my mother and aunt said I lied. Could you please kill the black insects?' I told her with firmness, 'Why not? But you have to obey my word'. Then I advised her to sing any song throughout the day. And by the grace of Music, she recovered.

These two instances added fuel me to my research in Music Therapy through Astrology. Then I wrote several articles in several magazines, which some astrologers and august persons in the field of Music highly appreciated. And some esteemed organisations honoured me with the title. Then I thought that if I wrote my findings in English, I could convey my work to many august persons other than Bengal. And, thus I completed this book now.

And I am now waiting for my valued readers' formative assessments and comments.

Dipchand Math, Basumitra Majumder
Sheoraphuli, Hooghly.

May 9, 2023

# Acknowledgments

In this work, and by this opportunity, I, greatfully, acknowledge a few personalities who helped me in this work and did their best to prepare this book.

Dr. Amalendu Sarkar (M.B.B.S., D.T.M & H, M.D, Consultant Physician & Chest Specialist)

Mr Abir Sen (Renowned Professor)

Mr Chinmoy Goswami (Renowned Educationist)

Mr Obhijit Chatterjee (Tagore thinker, Film maker)

Ms Debalina Mitra (Austin, USA)

Mrs Kumarika Majumder (My wife)

And the team of Notion Press

# Introduction of some Words used in this Book

The entire book uses all Bengali terms of Indian Music. Here, in brief, we would like to introduce them.

Abarohan = The descending order. As Sa'-Ni-Dha-Pa-Ma-Ga-Re-Sa.

Arohan = The ascending order. As Sa-Re-Ga-Ma-Pa-Dha-Ni-Sa'.

Barjita = Varjita, Absent. The excluded swar or note. The note which is not there or excluded from a raga.

Swar = svara, note. (Sa Re Ga Ma Pa Dha Ni or Do Re Mi Fa So La Si.)

Sa = C. Sadoj or Saroj, the first note (Swar) of Indian Music.

Re = D. Rekhab or Rishov, the second Swar of Indian Music.

Ga = E. Gandhar, the third Swar of Indian Music.

Ma = F. Madhyam, the fourth Swar of Indian Music.

Pa = G. Pancham, the fifth Swar of Indian Music.

Dha = A. Dhaibat, the sixth Swar of Indian Music.

Ni = B. Nishad or Nikhad, the seventh Swar of Indian Music.

Sa' = C of the upper octave.

Suddha = Natural swar as Sa, Re, Ga, Ma etc.

Komal = flat. We use lowercase to denote the flat (Komal) swar, like, re, ga, dha & ni.

Tibra = sharp. We use upper case to denote the sharp (Tibra) swar, like MA. In Indian Music, only Madhyam (MA) has the sharp swar.

Kodi = Tibra swar.

Pakad = The chain of swars by which we identify the raga.

Pakar = Pakad.

Saptak = A series of swars. Gamut. in European Music it is called Octave.

Rasa = Aesthetic flavour, sentiments.

Shadava = Shadav, Ragas consists of six swars at the time of Arohan & Abarohan.

Aurava = Odhav, Ragas consists five swars at the time of Arohan & Abarohan.

Aharatra = Entire day and night. 24 hours.

Purnima = Full Moon

Amabasya = New Moon

# A Rational Approach to Music Therapy

One latest news story has caused quite a stir. An unconscious patient has regained consciousness by listening to the Hindustani raga sangeet. The incident took place at the famous S.S.K.M. Hospital in Kolkata. The doctor was a violinist. Ever since the incident, the list of ragas used to cure disease has spread across Facebook and WhatsApp. And we found that, suddenly, as if by magic, the people of Bengal have woken from a deep sleep and become musicologists.

On this occasion, a few enthusiastic authors and publishers have released several books. In addition, some music teachers have started distributing visiting cards claiming to be music therapists. This temporary frenzy has arisen because science-conscious people have come to know that music can heal any patient.

But, in the true sense, the magic of the melody is not an unknown subject to us. From various legends, we learn that the tune of music affects not only human beings but also animals, even plants. For example, scientist Jagadish Chandra Bose showed in his research that when beautiful melodies are applied to plants, the growth and associated healing functions are easily enhanced. With this, he caused a stirrer in the world by discovering the 'kunchan rekha' (in Bengali, 'koonchan rekha'--- the curling line, as we find on the E.C.G. paper). Moreover, his Crescograph showed the movement of plants.

In the case of animals, we learn the influence of music and melody from Tanraj Tansen's story. Tansen was one of the jewels of the Navaratna Sabha of Emperor Akbar. He had subdued the mad elephant by singing. He lit the fire by singing the Deepak Raga. With the melody of the music, he brought the spring ceremony to a dry forest. We also heard about many musical qualities, which calmed people's minds with songs and even alleviated the pain of incurable diseases.

In this context, again, we can remember the incident in the interior courtyard of Emperor Akbar, where the princess suffered from an immedicable illness. When all the medicines of Hakim Sahib had failed to cure the princess's disease, then Hakim Sahib advised the court musicians to wash away the sickness with the flow of melody. And after listening to music, the princess healed from her sick bed.

In our ancient literature, we can find numerous illustrations in this regard. For example, we found that a morbid or severely weak person had been brought to the temple by villagers. Underneath the Almighty statue's feet, all the devotees sang together, singing in chorus, the Kirtan. And after a few moments or hours, the weak person recovered from his disease. The devotees claimed that God's grace recovered the person. But we are saying that he got well by the grace of music.

Even if we look at our previous days, we find a marvellous example of Indian music. Children's writer Punyalata Chakraborty said while reminiscing, "*Once Didi [Sukhlata, elder sister of Punyalata] fell very ill. Severe pain. No sleep in the eyes. Even sleeping pills also did not work. Usually, all parents will be shocked to see their daughter's suffering. But Upendrakishar [the famous writer, printer, artist & musicologist, and the father of Sukhlata] was not so upset; he calmly sat next to the girl. He started playing with the violin in hand. Sukhlata fell asleep listening to the music.*" (*Chhelebelar Dinguli by Punyolata Chakraborty, Pg. 81*)

We have heard in a lyric of Hindi Bhajan—

*Sangeet hay shakti Ishwar ki*

*Har sur me base hai Raam*

*Ragi yo shunaye raga Madhur*

*Rogi ko mile aaram.*

(Song is the power of God. In every tune, there dwelling Shree Raam - the Almighty, the singer sings the song, and the patient feels comfort [by listening to that song.])

So, by witnessing our glorious history, we can conclude that music therapy is not a new subject in India. But it has been suppressed by the jet paced lifestyle and income-oriented limited knowledge.

We have already mentioned the unconscious patient who was brought back to consciousness by listening to Hindustani classical music for a long time. The point is that music can vibrate the patient's nervous system. From that vibration, his consciousness gradually becomes active. The musical tune motivates to conduct the patient's nerve activity.

But we have not yet seen any reasonable discussion of how it works. I have discussed this with many people who have worked on it, but they could not give any reasonable explanation. The only comment is that this raga can cure that disease. So let's think of some rational thoughts and how to benefit people.

# How Music Acts

Music closely connects our body, mind, and nervous system. A child falls asleep to listen to the rhythm of the lullaby, swaying on the mother's lap. To induce his urine, his mother has given a whistling sound. And to cheer him up, we clap in front of him. For a child who is unable to move the organs of his own will, music alone helps him to function properly. These examples prove that music and rhythm influence a child's nervous system directly.

But as adults, they know they can control their emotions and organs with the help of their minds. But simultaneously, they can control their feelings according to the melody and rhythm. So, for example, if a young chap calls a 15-17-year-old girl 'aunty', she gets angry. But if a kid calls her 'aunty', the girl becomes enamoured and busy cuddling the child by hearing the tone, her manner of speech, the style of the address on the child's face, the instant latent motherhood in the girl's mind exudes the *Vatsalya rasa* (the aesthetic flavour rises from affection). Still, the same address by a young chap annoys her by reminding her of the failures of her adolescent life. So again, if somebody calls you by your name, screaming and repeating it, you will be disturbed repeatedly. But if a distressed man cries out as soon as you hear it, a feeling rises in your heart, and you start looking around, trying to figure out the sound from where it is coming.

Leaving people on the sidelines, suppose you have gone to a temple where animals are sacrificed. The beast has ascended the sacrifice post, and the sword is lifted to separate his head from the body. The animal's scream will disturb your spirit no matter how pious you were at the time. Even if you want to pretend not to hear it by being unmindful, your mind moves by that scream. And the scream of a slaughtered animal disturbs your mind because that tone and tune excite your nerves. As found in mythology, Kara-Nakara, Damama, and war music were performed on the battlefield to motivate the soldiers during the war. Similarly, music can control happiness, sadness, joy, excitement, and satisfaction.

Now, let's think about the cause of our emotional movement by listening to music, tune, or rhythm. Each song or each sound or rhythm, with the neural activity in our brain, helps to control the excretion of several glands. In this way, music is used to cure illnesses.

It is known that the leading cause of any disease is the secretion or some exudation, poor secretion, or excessive secretion or not. For example, a hyper acidic patient feels a burning sensation in the chest, or his stomach starts to feel bad. The reason for this burning sensation and pain is the secretion of the gastrin hormone. This hormone powerfully stimulates the gastric glands for the secretion of gastric juice. As a result, treatment of acidity is only possible if the cause of this secretion is found. We know that we should take antacids when we have acidity problems. But it can indeed relieve the disease, not cure it. Therefore, we must find the exact cause of gastrin or gastric hormonal secretion to heal. The patient can be cured only when the reason behind the malady is found.

There are various human diseases—infections, inflammations, secretion disorders, etc. According to Ayurveda, the source of all such diseases is Vayu-Pitta-Kapha within the human body. They are called 'Dhat'. According to Ayurveda, 'Dhat' is a body elixir. This 'dhat' means the principal cause. The illness's cause and the source may differ based on the Vayu-Pitta-Kapha principle. There are also variations in fever symptoms. Ayurvedic scriptures are said to prescribe such different methods of treatment.

We easily say one thing--- go to the doctor to cure the disease. The doctor examines the patient and diagnoses, then prescribes medicine and food. And by using that medicine and that food, the patient recovers. Somehow, the word 'cured' needs to be corrected. The disease is healed in two ways. One is in remission, while the other is curable. It is not clear if the patient was cured or relieved. Relief or remission means temporary suspension but not recovery. Healing is healing—the same holds for medicine, the proportion of food, and even music.

Now, our question is whether we cure people with music or cause a temporary break from illness and pain. In response to this question, certain conditions can be relieved by music. It is also possible to cure some diseases.

There are so many diseases where music is not able to do anything. For example, say someone has a boil or a portion of someone's body is cut and bleeding. In both cases, music cannot do any work. But pain, even if the pain is labour pain or bleeding from abnormal menstruation, can be relieved by music.

Only those diseases and ailments, and at the source of the illness where the human mind is active, those diseases that form by the cause of human mind waves may be cured by music. For example, blood pressure and uncontrolled secretion of hormones because of anxiety, depression, nervous tension, abnormal menstruation, labour pain etc. those types of disorders can be relieved if the human mind can be appeased and controlled.

If you want to cure a disease with music or rhythm, you need to understand which tune (Raga) can cure which disease and how that melody can affect the patient. If it does the opposite, it will not cure the disease but will do more harm, as we have seen in the case of allopathic medicine- which is especially important for a particular patient. However, many have recovered after taking that. It has also been observed that the same medication cannot work for some patients; instead, it has caused another problem by increasing the disease. The fact is that every person's constitution is different. Therefore, all medicines do not work equally in everyone's body.

For this reason, doctors try to know a patient's physical and mental structure and status before treatment. Especially before doing homoeopathy treatment, doctors ask the patient and the patient's party various questions. Then, knowing all the information, they arrange to prescribe the medicine.

# Short Notes on Indian Astrology

Before the music-therapeutic discussion, let's explore the astrological field shortly. In this chapter, we are saying something about Indian Astrology so that all the readers of this book can understand the subject discussed here.

In Indian Astrology, there are twelve signs: Aries, Taurus, Gemini, Cancer, Leo, Virgo, Libra, Scorpio, Sagittarius, Capricorn, Aquarius, and Pisces.

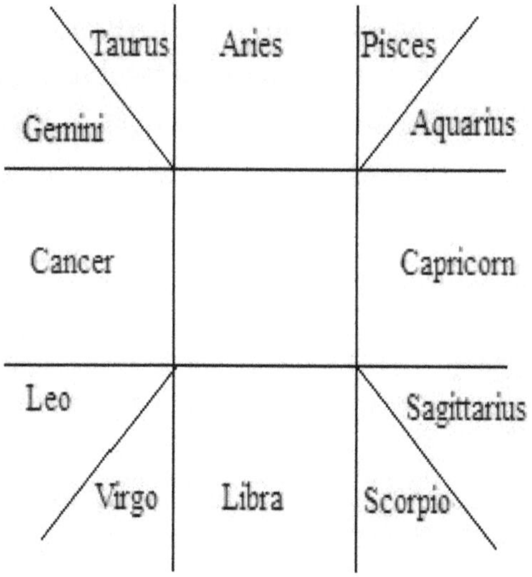

And has nine planets: Sun, Moon, Mars, Mercury, Jupiter, Venus, Saturn, Rahu (Dragons Head) and Ketu (Dragons Tail). Rahu and Ketu denote the points of intersection of the Sun and Moon paths as they move on the celestial sphere. Therefore, Rahu and Ketu are respectively called the north and the south lunar nodes. But in Indian astrology, these two are honoured as Planets.

Other than these nine, there are another three planets, namely Uranus, Neptune and Pluto. Although In August 2006, the International Astronomical Union (IAU) downgraded the status of Pluto to that of a 'dwarf planet.'

We know that there are many points to argue against the planets of Astrology. But we are going differently. Here we are just informing the name of twelve signs and nine planets of Indian Astrology. So, leaving that argument aside, let us move the discussion forward.

The Sun, Moon, Mars, Mercury, Jupiter, Venus and Saturn these seven planets acquire twelve signs.

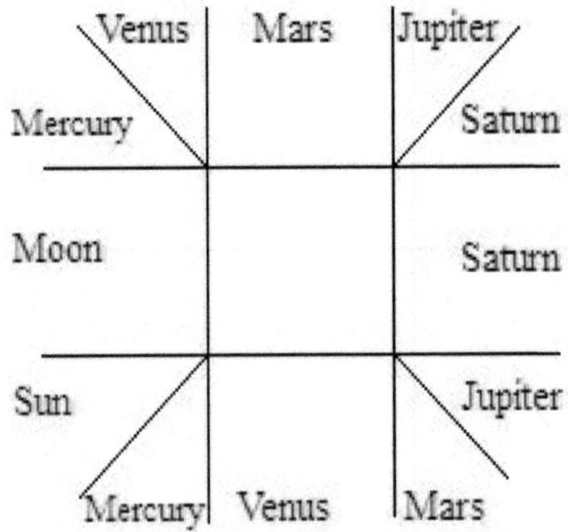

The Sun situates or acquires Leo, and the Moon acquires Cancer. And another five planets take the places of two signs each. Like Mars acquires Aries and Scorpio, Mercury acquires Gemini and Virgo, Jupiter acquires Sagittarius and Pisces, Venus acquires Taurus and Libra, and Saturn acquires Capricorn and Aquarius signs.

Now we are like to introduce the zodiac chart. A circle means 360 Degrees. In this 360 Degree, twelve signs are situated. So each sign acquires 360/12 = 30 Degrees. So let's draw a zodiac chart of these twelve signs according to the East Indian style.

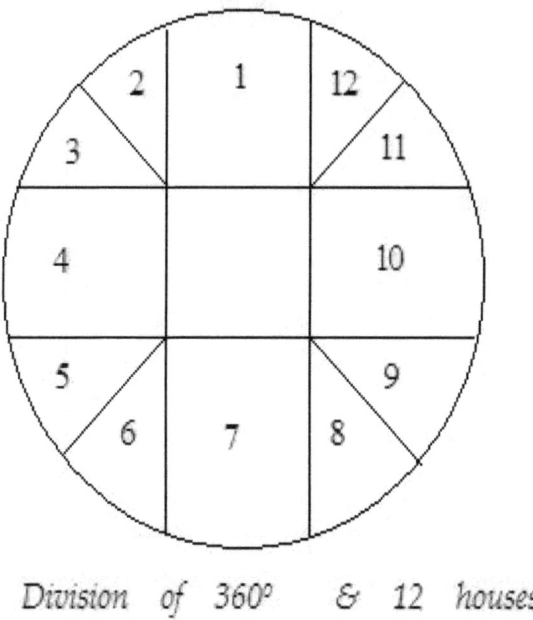


*Division of 360° & 12 houses*

And as per North Indian as well as popular to other than East Indian style, the chart is as below:

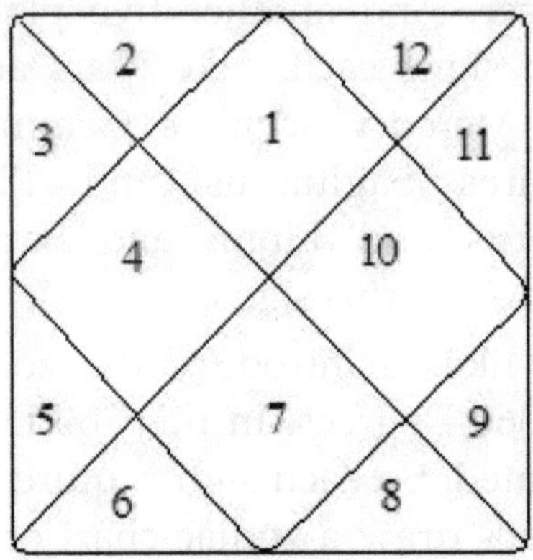


*Divition of 360° & 12 houses (North Indian Style)*

And the position of Rashis as per North Indian style is as below:

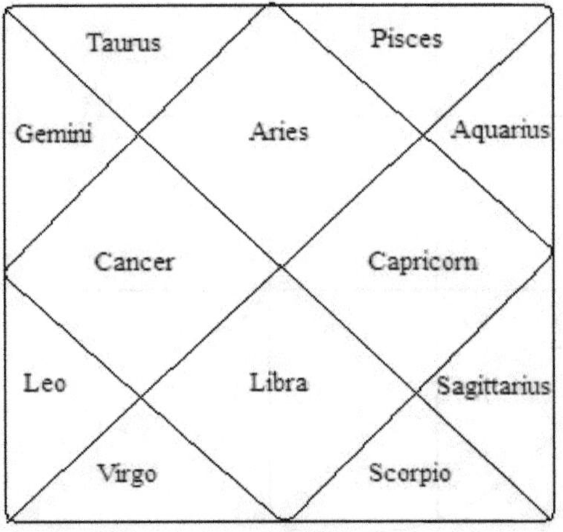


*Signs position as per North Indian Style*

The particular house of sign (Rashi) and planets show below:

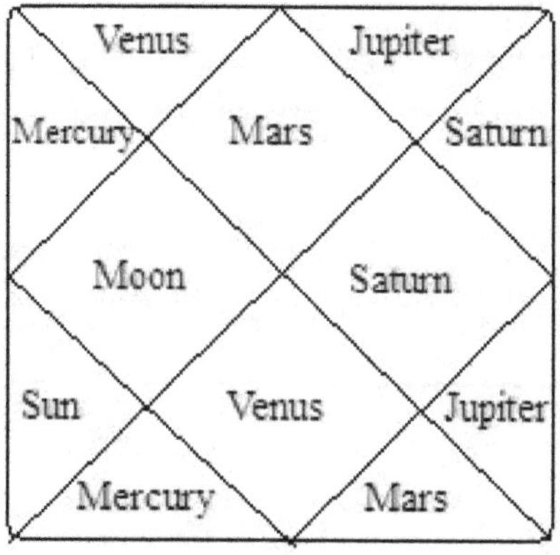


*Planetary position as per North Indian Style*

We have already been told that the Sun, Moon, Mars, Mercury, Jupiter, Venus and Saturn are seven planets that acquire twelve signs. So let's draw another chart. This chart is very particularly important to our discussion.

In the entire discussion, we will draw the chart per Eastern Indian.

Taurus Venus
Aries Mars
Pisces Jupiter
Gemini Mercury
Aquarius Saturn
Cancer Moon
Capricorn Saturn
Leo Sun
Sagittarius Jupiter
Virgo Mercury
Libra Venus
Scorpio Mars

Another point is that, in our picture, we considered Aries the first house of the zodiac chart. But at the birth chart examination time, we would think of the ascendant (*Lagna*) as the first house. Then we count anti-clockwise second, third, fourth etc. houses.

| Taurus 2 / Gemini 3 | Aries *Asc* 1 | Pisces 12 / Aquarius 11 |
|---|---|---|
| Cancer 4 | | Capricorn 10 |
| Leo 5 / 6 Virgo | 7 Libra | 8 Scorpio / Sagittarius 9 |

*Ascendant is Aries*

And in the entire discussion, we will mention the 'sign' according to the Indian astrological system, i,e. 'Rashi'. The concepts of the Western zodiac sign and the Indian Rashi are entirely different. Western zodiac sign stands on the Sun's position. But in the Indian system, it relies on the Moon. The Sun stays more or less one month in a sign. So in the Western system, all people born in the same month have the same sign. But according to the Indian astrological system, the Rashi depends on the Moon's position in the zodiac. Moon stays in a sign only for 54 hours. So from the beginning to the end of a Rashi, it is only 54 hours. And in the entire discussion, the term 'Rashi' or 'sign' should be understood as the zodiac sign according to the Indian system.

# Musical Swars and Planets

Now let's discuss a matter which has not, as we consider, been discussed before in the field of Indian music. Some Indian musicologists have rarely addressed the glimpse of emotion, colour, and the glimpse of the atmosphere of swar. But they never discussed the influence or role of planets on the swar, tune, and rhythm of Indian music. In a book of astrology, "*Bharate Jyotishcharcha O Kosthi-bicharer Sutraboli*" by Sri Narendranath Bagal, we find a little paragraph in a chapter '*Pancham-bhab Bichar*' (consideration of the fifth house) containing merely six or seven lines where the author gave some indication on it. After reading the paragraph, we feel interested in discussing it. In that paragraph, the author referred to a note based on Pythagorean Astrological consideration, where Pythagoras considered the seven swars influenced by seven planets.

Pythagoras, apart from being a great philosopher, mathematician, scientist, and anthropologist, is also considered a musicologist of ancient Greek. He was the pioneer of the notation of music in Europe. He was a great astronomer and astrologist also. And the founder of '*Musica Universalis*' (literally universal music) means the harmony of the spheres. An ancient philosophical concept regards proportions in the movements of celestial bodies, the Sun, the Moon, Mars, and other planets, as a form of music. This 'music' is not thought to be audible but rather a harmonic mathematical or religious resonance. And he also believed that the seven swars, C, D, E, F, G, A, and B, are influenced by seven planets like the Sun, Saturn, Mercury, Moon, Mars, Venus, and Jupiter, respectively. And he made a chart based on that. So in the opinion of Pythagoras, the seven swars of music are ruled by the seven planets. As per his concept, musical swar C is influenced by the Sun, Saturn influences D, Mercury influences E, F is influenced by the Moon, Mars influences G, Venus influences A, and Jupiter influences B.

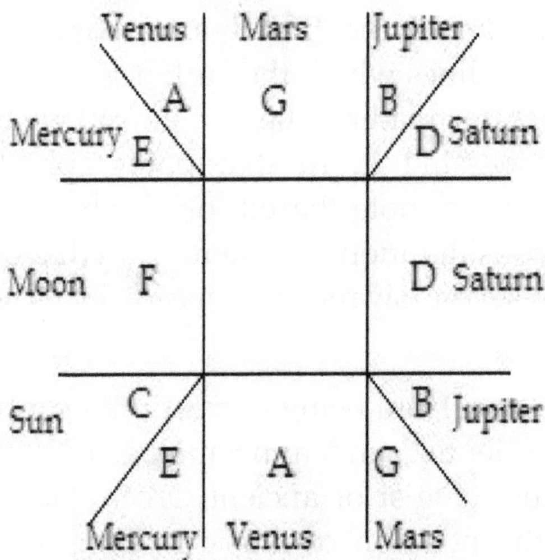


*Position of musical notes as per Pythagoras*

In Indian Music, C is called Sa (Sadoj / Saroj), D is called Re (Rekhab / Rishav), E is called Ga (Gandhar), F is called Ma (Madhyam), G is called Pa (Pancham), A is called Dha (Dhaibat), and B is called Ni (Nishad/Nikhad).

There are some differences between European music and Indian music. In European music, every swar has its natural, sharp, and flat conditions. In Indian music, 'sharp' is called '*Tibra*', and 'flat' means '*Komal*'. According to European notation, C swar stands with his natural, sharp, and flat conditions. We can find the order of sharps as F sharp, C sharp, G sharp, D sharp, A sharp, E sharp, B sharp, and the order of flats is the reverse of the order of sharps: B flat, E flat, A flat, D flat, G flat, C flat, F flat. But in the Indian musical system, only Re (D), Ga (E), Dha (A), and Ni (B) have *Komal* (flat) and natural both swars and Ma (F) have natural and *Tibra* (sharp) swars. But Sa and Pa stand only on natural swar. In respect of this condition of swars, we cannot accept the Pythagorean Laws of planetary influence on musical swars, undoubtedly. So we are like to introduce a new chart of planetary influences on the chromatic swars or twelve-swars. In this chart, we are considering that Sa (C) is influenced by Sun, Re (D) is influenced by Saturn, Ga (E) is influenced by Mercury, Ma (F) is influenced by Mars, and Moon influences Pa (G), Venus influences Dha (A), Ni (B) is influenced by Jupiter.

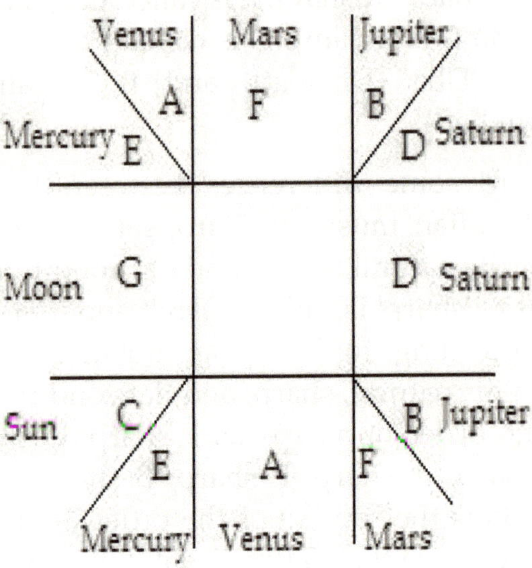


*Position of musical notes as per introduced chart*

There are some differences between Pythagorean and our contemplated chart, especially in the swars of Ma (F) and Pa (G). Pythagoras considered Ma (F) influenced by the Moon and Pa (G) by Mars. But we contemplate that Ma (F) is influenced by Mars and Pa (G) by the Moon. Because in Indian music, Pa (G) stands only on unalterable natural swar. But Ma (F) has its natural and sharp swars. According to the zodiac chart, Mars has two houses, but the Moon has only one place.

To prepare the new chart, we focus especially on the unalterable natural swars of Sa (C) and Pa (G) as the Sun and the Moon, respectively. If we think about both, the music has seven *Suddha* swars (natural swars) and five *Bikrita* swaras (flat & sharp swars), totalling twelve swars. These twelve are called chromatic swars. Let's draw a chart with twelve swars. Here we consider natural C, D, E, F, G, A, & B as Sa, Re, Ga, Ma, Pa, Dha, and Ni, respectively. And *Komal* (flat) swars as re, ga, dha, ni and *Tibra* or *Kodi* (sharp) Madhyam as MA. Further saying that we have invented the position of all *Bikrito* (flat & sharp) swars.

| Dha, Ga, A, E | Ma, F, G | ni, Bb, re, Db |
|---|---|---|
| Pa, G, *F* | | D, Re |
| Sa, C, Eb, ga | Ab, dha | B, F#, Ni, MA, G |

*Position of swars. Pythagorean swars are in italics.*

*'Db', 'Eb', 'Ab' & 'Bb' means the flat note or Komal swar, i.e., Komal re, Komal ga, Komal dha, Komal ni, respectively. And 'F#' means sharp note or Tibra Madhyam (MA) swar.*

In astrology, we found twelve signs and seven planets. And these seven planets acquire twelve signs. However, only two planets acquire one sign each. Namely, the sun and the moon take Leo and Cancer signs, respectively. And another five, each occupies with two signs. So, to put it bluntly, in the zodiac system, the Sun and the Moon have only one house,

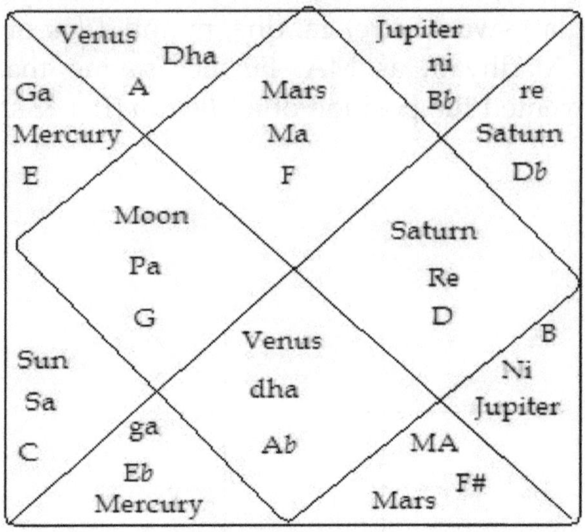


*Position of swars (North Indian Style)*

but Mars, Mercury, Jupiter, Venus, and Saturn have two places each. So now, we can draw a zodiac chart with the name of chromatic swars. (Seven natural swars and five bikrita or alterable swars).

## II

As we said, there are twelve planets in astrology: the Sun, the Moon, Mars, Mercury, Jupiter, Venus, Saturn, Rahu (Dragon's head), Ketu (Dragon's tail), Uranus, Neptune, and Pluto. In this series, Rahu, Ketu, Uranus, Neptune, and Pluto are not the ruling planet. So in a zodiac chart, astrology believes that only seven planets rule over twelve signs. Each planet stands for many sentiments and emotions.

The **Sun** is the soul. The Sun stands for light, lustre, seriousness, self-expression, self-manifestation, vigour, courage, pity, religious sense, Infinity, divine love, will force, respect, dignity, etc. In the adverse, arrogance, pride, and unrest.

The **Moon** is the mind. The Moon governs imagination, personality, peace, hardness, firmness, and tenderness. And in the adverse, dissatisfaction, cowardice, timidness, restlessness, etc.

**Mars** stands for materialism, philosophy, action, war, courage, atheism, scepticism, egoism, heroic activities, etc. In the adverse low confidence, doubtful, fearful, perverse, rogue, and irreligious.

**Mercury** especially stands for intellect. It also governs memory, analysis, criticism, presence of mind, rationality, patience, intelligence, proper judgment, opinion, etc. The opposing stands for stupidity, foolishness, talkative or garrulous, crazy, etc.

**Jupiter** stands for morality, justice, equality, optimism, honesty, progress, progeny, philosophy, religion, wisdom, education, spirituality, idealism, devotion, etc. In the adverse hypocrite, atheist, misbeliever, faithless, etc.

**Venus** governs luxury, aesthetics, love, harmony, sympathy, embellishment, pleasure, romanticism, etc. In the adverse Luxuriant, unpopularity, unattractive etc.

**Saturn** governs poverty, misfortune, hindrance, impersonality, old age, philosophy, religion, asceticism, and occultism. In the adverse laziness, discouragement, impatience, restlessness, and apathy.

In Indian music, the number of swars is twelve, which we have told earlier, Sa, Re, Ga, Ma, Pa, Dha, Ni– these are the seven natural swars. And re, ga, dha, and ni are the *Komal* (flat) swar, and MA is the *Tibra* (sharp) swar. So, along with natural, flat & sharp swars, the chromatic swars are twelve. So, in the entire article, we would use Sa, Re, Ga, Ma, Pa, Dha, Ni as natural C, D, E, F, G, A, B and re, ga, dha, ni as D flat, E flat, A flat, B flat and MA as F sharp. So, if we arrange the twelve swars accordingly, it will show as Sa, re, Re, ga, Ga, Ma, MA, Pa, dha, Dha, ni, Ni.

In Indian music, the Sa (C) and Pa (G) swars are always only in unalter natural conditions, and another five swars have natural and *Bikrito* (flat and sharp) conditions. Earlier, we told that as in Indian music, basic swars are seven, and in Astrology, seven planets acquire two signs. Among them, each of the five planets had acquired two signs. Those five planets are Mars, Mercury, Jupiter, Venus, and Saturn. But the Sun and the Moon always acquire only one sign each. Hence the planets of the zodiac chart are serially arranged as Mars, Venus, Mercury, Moon, Sun, Mercury, Venus, Mars, Jupiter, Saturn, Saturn, and Jupiter, respectively. And the chromatic swars Ma, Dha, Ga, Pa, Sa, ga, dha, MA, Ni, Re, re, and ni are influenced by those seven planets. Let's draw a picture.

| | | |
|---|---|---|
| Taurus<br>Venus<br>Dha<br>A<br>Gemini<br>Mercury<br>Ga E | Aries<br>Mars<br>Ma<br>F | Pisces<br>Jupiter<br>ni<br>Bb<br>Saturn<br>Aquarius<br>re Db |
| Cancer<br>Moon<br>Pa G | | Capricorn<br>Saturn<br>Re D |
| Leo<br>Sun<br>Sa<br>C<br>Eb<br>ga<br>Mercury<br>Virgo | Ab<br>dha<br>Venus<br>Libra | Sagittarius<br>B Ni<br>Jupiter<br>F#<br>MA<br>Mars<br>Scorpio |

*Planetary influence of swars with signs*

This picture shows that Sa is influenced by the Sun, and the Moon influences Pa. Therefore, the nature of the Sun takes place in the swar Sa. The nature of the Moon takes place in the swar Pa. And, the nature of Mars appears at Ma and MA, the nature of Mercury appears at Ga and ga; likewise, the character of Jupiter at Ni and ni, the nature of Venus at Dha and dha, and the nature of Saturn are appeared at Re and re.

## III

In this chapter, before we enter our discussion, we should explore a few similarities between astrological and musical rules.

In the solar system, the Sun has a leading and vital role. We know that the Sun is the creator of this world. In Indian music, as per the opinion of some musicologists, all other six swars are generated from Sa (C). Therefore, we can say that the Sa is the same important swar as the Sun.

According to another opinion, Ma is the mother of all swars of the Octave. In the '*Archik era*' (the earlier period of the Vedas), there was only one swar. That swar was 'Ma'. From Ma, the other six swars gradually generated. According to the Indian emotion and in the Indian language, 'Ma' means Mother. As the mother gives birth to the child, 'Ma' generates the other swars of music. But, we think, as per musical terms, 'Ma' stands for 'Madhyam', the middle position. Before 'Ma', there are three swars (Sa, Re, Ga), and after 'Ma', another three swars (Pa, Dha, Ni). Sa is immensely important in music. As the world becomes meaningless without the Sun, Indian music can create no songs or ragas without the swar Sa.

| Sa | Re | Ga | **Ma** | Pa | Dha | Ni |
|---|---|---|---|---|---|---|

*Position of Ma*

In the zodiac-chart Moon is the next important planet after the Sun. Likewise, 'Pa' or Pancham is the next important swar in Indian music.

As we know, the Full Moon, New Moon, tide, and even the discrimination of blood pressure and arthritis pain depend upon the attraction and repulsion of the Sun and the Moon. In music, Sa and Pa control the emotions like this.

As per the astrological view, the Kendra (centre) and the Kone or Trikone (triangular) positions are significant. The planets situated to the distance of ninety ($90^0$) degrees, one hundred eighty ($180^0$) degrees, two hundred seventy ($270^0$) degrees, and three hundred and sixty ($360^0$) degrees or zero ($0^0$) are called the *Kendra* (centre). That means the First, Fourth, Seventh & Tenth houses are called the Kendra (centre). And the distance of one hundred twenty ($120^0$) degrees and two hundred forty ($240^0$) degrees is called *Kone / Trikone* (Triangular). In simple words, the Fifth and the Ninth houses are called Kone. According to this law, we can observe that Ma is the fourth swar of Sa, and Pa is the fifth. Again, Sa-Pa-Sa' (Sa' means the Sa of Taar saptak, the next of Mudara saptak.) is situated at the fifth and the fourth position accordingly.

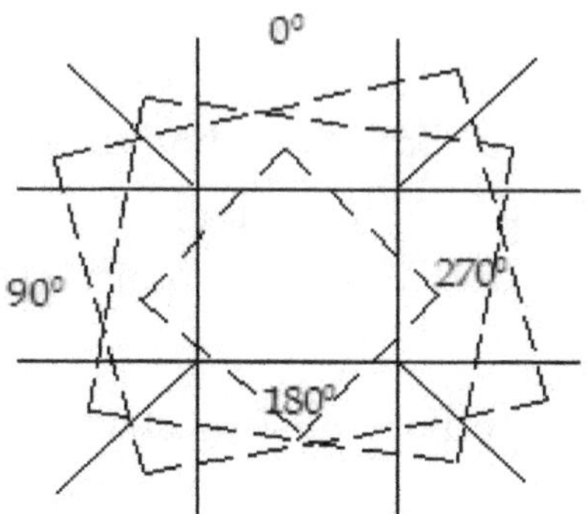


*Position of Kendra or Centre*

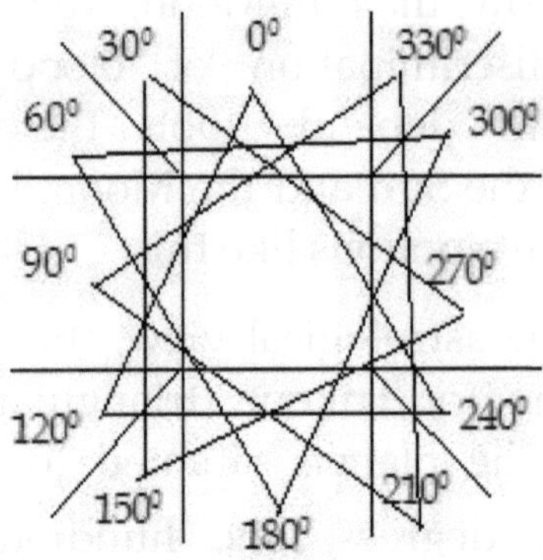


*Position of Kone/Trikone or Triangle*

In India, the gamut or the seven notes of classical music is called '*Saptak*', also known as register. But in western systems, C, D, E, F, G, A, B and C, these eight notes are taken as one register, called 'Octave'. So we consider here *saptak* and octave as the same term. There are three prime *saptaks* used in Indian music. The lower *saptak* is called the *Mandra saptak* or lower octave, the Middle and the basic *saptak* is *Mudara* or *Madhya saptak,* and the Higher octave is called the *Taar saptak.*

If we look at the planets in the zodiac, we can find that Mars, the planet of Ma (the natural Madhyam), situates at two hundred forty ($240^0$) degrees from the Sun (the planet of Sa). And the Sun is situated one hundred twenty ($120^0$) degrees from Mars. So that means both placed after the ninth & fifth angular distance.

As per the zodiac musical chart, the natural Re (*rekhab*) situates at one hundred eighty ($180^0$) degrees from Pa (*Pancham*), which swar is influenced by the

Moon. On the other hand, the *Komal* re (D# flat) situates at one hundred eighty ($180^0$) degree distance from the Sa (Sadoj), which swar influenced by Sun.

According to astronomical rules, when the Sun and the Moon situate at one hundred eighty ($180^0$) degrees from each other, then a Full Moon (*Purnima*) occurs. And when both situate at zero ($0^0$) degrees, it is called a New Moon (*Amavasya*). The brightness of the Moon develops when Moon is situated at one hundred eighty ($180^0$) degrees from the Sun; both take place on the opposite side or face to face with each other. Because of the face-to-face position, they can enjoy their journey of focus and the convergence of light straightly. This system is also applicable in the case of music. Sa and re (*Komal rekhab*) are situated just one hundred eighty ($180^0$) degrees from each other.

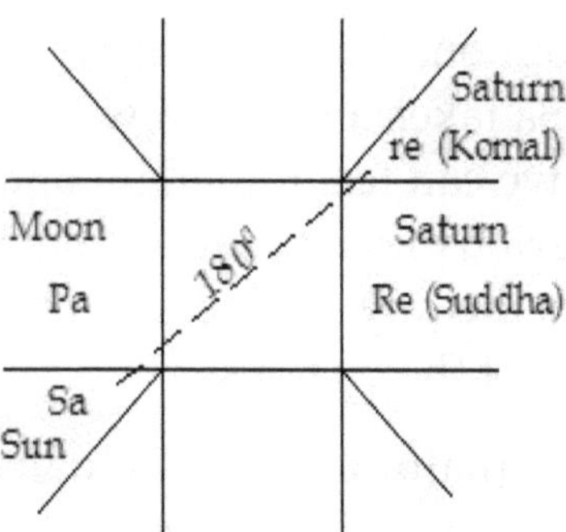


*Komal re situates at 180° from the Sun*

For this reason, there emanates the magnificent tune, which makes our minds apathetic and insensible. We feel an excellent seriousness from these two swars, which grow from the navel and inspire us to expand our spiritual thoughts.

Because the Sun influences the Sa and Saturn influences re, this is the main reason or vital mystery for developing this thought. We discussed earlier that the Sun stands for light, lustre, seriousness, self-expression, vigour, courage, pity, religious sense, Infinity, divine love, will force, respect, dignity, etc. And Saturn governs poverty, misfortune, hindrance, impersonality, old age, philosophy, religion, asceticism, and occultism. So by the union of these two planets, we feel the seriousness, courage, religious sense, Infinity, divine love, will force, respect, dignity, and impersonality in our minds. Especially for this reason, all the morning ragas are like Vairo. Bhairavi, Ramkeli, and Lalit notice this type of feeling.

On the other hand, when this re (*Komal rekhab*) wants to come as close as possible to the Sun or moves afar from one hundred eighty (180) degrees to the Sun, then Sa takes a position with *suddha* (natural) Re. And then we can feel impatient and restless in the absence of seriousness because the Sun is slowly getting old. As the day progresses, men become busy with the agility of the business.

The *Suddha* (natural) Re is situated face to face (one hundred eighty ($180^0$) degrees) with Pa, the Moon. The Sun is the king of the day, and the Moon is the queen of the night. So, as the day progresses to the night, the Re (*rekhab*) expresses his business agility. This agility is not restlessness but, after meditation and worship, as the ascetic immersed in his daily work calmly and gravely. That emotion is the composition of softness, hardness, dissatisfaction, peace, quietness, indetermination, unrest, and timidness, along with the feelings of Re as well as Saturn, like apathetic discouragement.

In the year 1940, 'All India Radio' broadcast a marvellous talk show with songs by the direction of Kazi Nazrul Islam on 22nd June. The heading was '*Yam Yojonay Kodi Madhyam.*' That means the function of *Tibra* (sharp) *Madhyam* (MA) in the part of a period of three hours. '*Yam*' means three hours. There are eight *yams* in a whole day or 24 hours. Poet Kazi Nazrul Islam proved in that show that the *Kodi Madhyam* (MA) plays a vital part in changing the emotion when the time goes from one '*Yam*' to the next. Our findings show that the MA (*Kodi/Tibra Madhyam*) situates in the Scorpio sign. This Scorpio situates in the fourth house from the Sun and the fifth from the Moon.

On the other hand, *suddha Madhyam* (Ma) is situated at the Aries sign, at the ninth house from the Sun and the tenth house from the Moon. For this reason, Ma and MA take part in changing the emotions of the whole day. When *suddha Madhyam* (Ma) situates near the Sa (*Sadoj*) as well as the Sun, the emotion of Mars, like action, war, courage, scepticism, heroic activities, etc., grows. And on the other hand, when it relates to the Moon as well as pancham (Pa), it expresses the emotion of egoism, anger, sexual desire, etc. And *Tibra Madhyam* (MA) is an emotion like dissatisfaction, fluctuation, pain, inability, etc.

Venus's full influence is on the *suddha Dhaibat* (Dha) swar. For this reason, Dha indicates soft emotions like aesthetics, love, harmony, sympathy, embellishment, pleasure, and romanticism in the mind of a human being. And *Komal* dha bears the emotion like platonic love. So if the Dha (Venus) joins Ma (Mars), this combination develops love's excessive excitement. But the combination of Ma and Pa (Mars and Moon) always expresses the emotion of courage, heroism, firmness, etc.

The *suddha* (natural) *Gandhara* (Ga) and *Komal* (flat) *Gandhara* (ga) swars are influenced by Mercury and always manifest analysis, criticism, presence of mind, rationality, patience, intelligence, etc. In any tune made without Ga, there must be an adverse condition of emotions like stupidity, foolishness, talkativeness or garrulousness, craziness, etc.

The *Suddha* and *Komal Nishad* (Ni, ni) conduct religious emotion. Because Saturn influences Ni and ni, they control permanent emotions like patience, quiet, righteousness, excellence, impersonality, etc.

This was an outline of the planetary influence of the seven swars of Indian music.

IV

Now we would like to discuss the role of planets on Indian ragas. This chapter considers the word 'raga' for all raga and raginis. Let's start with Bhairavi raga.

**Bhairavi:** The universal poet Rabindranath Tagore said, "*Bhairavi is the pain of eternal separation of the* *lonely Infinite."* [*'Sangeeter Mukti', "Sangeet Chinta"*]. The Infinite is one and peerless. So his pain of eternal separation falls to the tune of Bhairavi.

As per the musical theory, the emotion of this raga is indifferent, sober, self-manifesting, and with some religious sense. The permanent emotion of this raga is soberness.

According to the theory of music, the *Vadi* (main) swar of Bhairavi is 'Ma', and the *Samvadi* (next to the main) swar is 'Sa'. The re, ga, dha & ni all are *Komal* (flat). In *Arohon* (ascending) contains Sa, re, ga, Ma, Pa, dha, ni, Sa'; and in *Abarohon* (descending), Sa', ni, dha, Pa, Ma, ga, re, Sa.

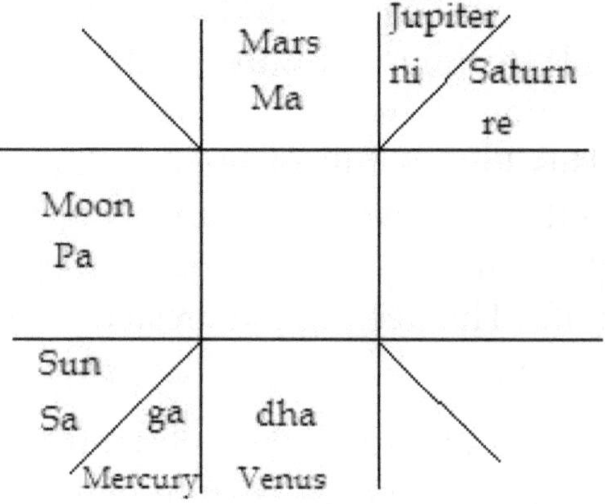


*Planetary position of Bhairabi's Arohon*

As we discussed, the Sa is the Sun, which means the Sa is self-manifestation. After Sa, the re swar vibrates from the navel of the belly bottom. The situation of those two swars takes our minds to Infinity. The navel is the main centre of our meditation or worship.

Our pursuit is to send air from *Kulakundalini* (the mystical circle- lying between the anus and the organ of generation) to the *Brahmarandhra*. The Sa and re of Bhairavi raga awaken that holy breathing. After Sa and re, there is *Komal Gandhara* (ga), which is influenced by the Mercury and manifests the decision, analysis, criticism, proper judgment, etc. After ga, there is Ma, which is ruled by Mars. This Ma gives self-confidence. Next is Pa, the swar of the Moon. This Pa controls our mind where the indescribable or heavenly feeling blooms after the start of the holy breathing. Then in the *Arohon* (Ascending), there are dha and ni swars. In these two swars, dha is influenced by Venus, the bloomer of platonic love (the love without sex and desire). This love is dwelling with *Komal* ni and arises the apathy and the spiritual feeling by the influence of Saturn. Combination of these two dha and ni arising divine love. This love is full of mental state, fear of losing after getting it. Every human being is a part of the Almighty, but they bear the pain of separation in their whole life. This feeling manifested in the dha and ni of Bhairavi raga.

For this reason, the permanent emotion of Bhairavi raga is peace or tranquillity. So that if all twelve swars applied to this raga, then its permanent emotion would be unchangeable. Even if the *Tibra madhyam* (MA) is applied to this raga, then the swinging or fluctuating emotion of MA is also unable to change its permanent sentiment. The main reason for this unchangeable emotion is the combination of Sa and *Komal* re swars.

**Hambeer:** *Arohon* (ascending) of Hambeer contains Sa Re Sa, Ga Ma Dha, Ni Dha, Ni Sa'; and *Abarohon* (descending) Sa'Ni DhaPa, MAPa DhaPa, Ga Ma Re Sa.

| Venus Dha<br>Ga Mercury | Mars Ma | |
|---|---|---|
| Moon Pa | | Saturn Re |
| Sun Sa | | Jupiter Ni<br>MA Mars |

*Planetary position of Raga Hambeer*

Dha is the *Vadi* swar of Hambeer raga. Dha means Venus, the planet of love, affection, and soft sentiment. The tune's main chain (*Pakad*) is Ga, Ma, and Dha. That means Mercury, Mars, and Venus. The combination of three emotions of Mars, Mercury, and Venus, i.e., courage, self-confidence, and soft sentiment. In this raga, we feel that our mind perceives discretion before being floated by the emotions of love, affection, etc.

For this reason, the emotion of this raga is free from the fault of lewdness. But the feeling of love is unavoidable because of the combination of Mars and Venus. And the presence of Ga, the Mercury, that love is honest. Therefore, musicologists said that this raga is the creator of *shringar* (love and beauty) and can also insist on the emotion of courage because a social servant may be a revolutionist or a hero when his love is honest.

**Hindol:** If we think about raga Hindol side by side, then we find that the *Vadi* (main) swar of Hindol is Dha and *Samvadi* (second or another primary or next to main) is Ga. That means love and wisdom are the fundamental nature of this raga. But according to the opinion of the musicologists, this raga is lustful. The character of Hindol is deceitful. In the picture of this raga, the hero is swinging on a hanging bed surrounded by so many pretty women. And musicology says that the love of the raga Hindol is not sincere or honest.

The cause of that emotion in Hindol is the absence of Re and Pa. The Re is influenced by Saturn, which gives feelings of devotion and faith. And Pa is ruled

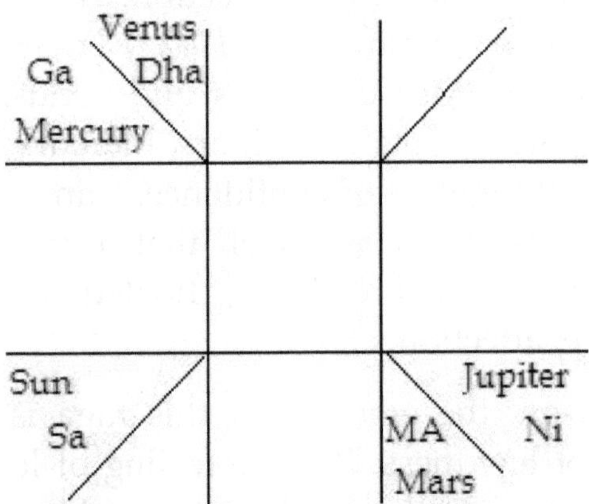

*Planetary position of Hindol's Arohon*

by the Moon. The Moon is the factor of mind. In this raga, Re and Pa are *Barjita* (excluded). So, although the Dha and Ga (the Venus and the Mercury) are the main swars, in other words, love and honesty are the main elements of this raga. This raga is deceitful due to the absence of Pa and Re as well as the mind and faithfulness. The *Arohon* (ascending order) of Hindol is Sa Ga MA Dha Ni Dha Sa', and *Abarohon* (descending order) is Sa' Ni Dha MA Ga Sa.

**Khambaj:** *Arohon* of Khambaj is Sa Ga Ma Pa Dha Ni Sa', and *Abarohon* is Sa' ni Dha Pa Ma Ga Re Sa.

The nature of Khambaj raga is restless. This raga's Vadi swar is Ga, and the Samvadi swar is Ni. That means Mercury is the main influence, and Jupiter is this raga's next main influential swar; Suddha Ni and Komal ni, both nishad (Ni), are used simultaneously in this raga. That means Jupiter of the sign Sagittarius

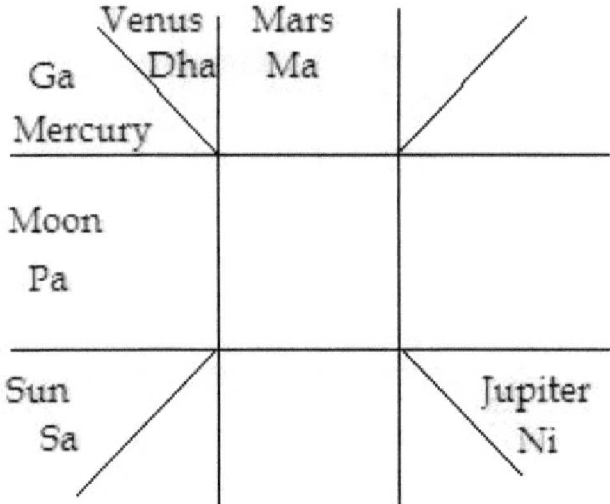


*Planetary position of Khambaj's Arohan*

and Pisces are the main ruling planets of this raga. As we stated earlier, Jupiter stands for morality, justice, equality, optimism, honesty, philosophy, religion, wisdom, and self-consciousness. So, although self-consciousness and morality are the main elements of this raga, due to the absence of the Re at the time of arohan (ascending), partial honesty is absent from the feeling, so the nature of this raga becomes restless.

**Kamod:** The *Arohon* of Kamod is SaRe, Pa, MAPaDhaPa, NiDhaSa', and *Abarohon* is Sa'ni DhaPa, MAPa GaMaPa, GaMa ReSa.

The *Vadi* swar of the raga Kamod is Pa, and the *Samvadi* swar is Re. Although the Re is the Samvadi swar of raga Kamod, the nature of this raga is also restless. If we think about it, we find that in Kamod, the Ni and Ga are very weak. As we know, the Ni and Ga are influenced by Jupiter and Mercury, respectively. These two planets consider self-consciousness, morality, religion, wisdom, etc. These

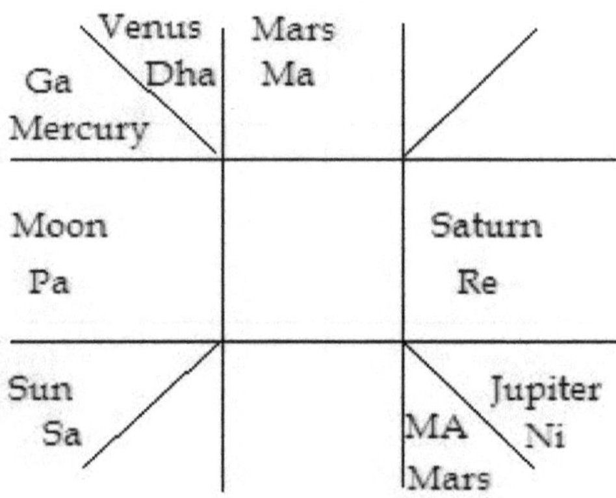


*Planetary position of Raga Kamod*

two planets are weak, meaning the feelings of religious, moral, and self-consciousness are weak or absent. Both the *Suddha* and *Tibra madhyam* (Ma & MA) are used in this raga. This *Tibra madhyam* (MA) denotes the Mars of the zodiac sign Scorpio. The nature of this Mars is self-confident but full of indecision mentality. For this reason, the indecision mentality, along with poor self-consciousness and morality, make its nature restless. Again, this indecision or oscillation nature of MA in raga Kamod brings the atmosphere of spring and love to mind.

**Todi (Tori):** The permanent emotion of raga Todi is *biprolombho shringer* (fear of separation at the time of union), or disappointment, a feeling of love or desire. The exhaustion, which is the emotion of raga Todi is nothing but the melancholy of impersonality as dissatisfaction and fatigue emotion occurs in the mind of heroin at the time of separation from his lover. That timid and melancholy impersonality is one kind of emotion of raga Todi.

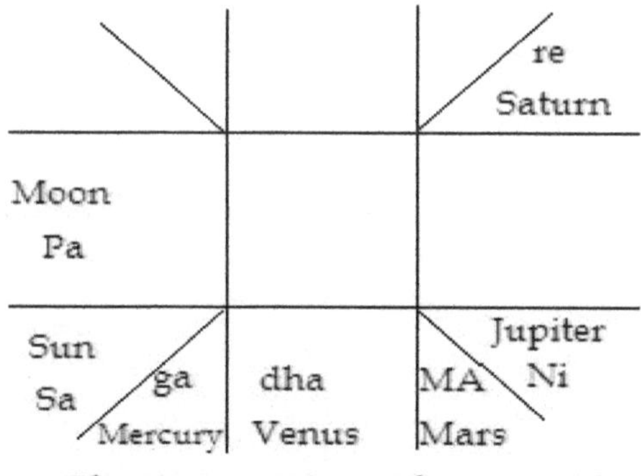


*Planetary position of Raga Todi*

The *Vadi* swar of raga Todi is Dha, and *Samvadi* is Ga. This raga builds up with *Komal* re, *Komal* ga, *Komal* dha, and *Tibra* MA (re, ga, dha, MA). As per our consideration, the main emotion of the *Vadi* swar is Dha, which means Venus, the love. And the *Samvadi* swar is Ga, which means Mercury, the ruler of decision, intelligence, wisdom, etc. The *Komal* re, ga, dha, and *Tibra* MA represent the planets Saturn, Mercury, Venus, and Mars, respectively. Those planets give misfortune, impersonality, laziness, discouragement of Saturn, the decision, intelligence, wisdom of Mercury, love, affection, soft sentiments of Venus, and indecision or oscillation nature by the influence of Mars. The combination of those emotions makes the lover an apathetic, separated single.

**Multani:** Like raga Todi, the re, ga, dha & MA swars are also used in the raga Multani. But there is some difference in emotions between these two ragas.

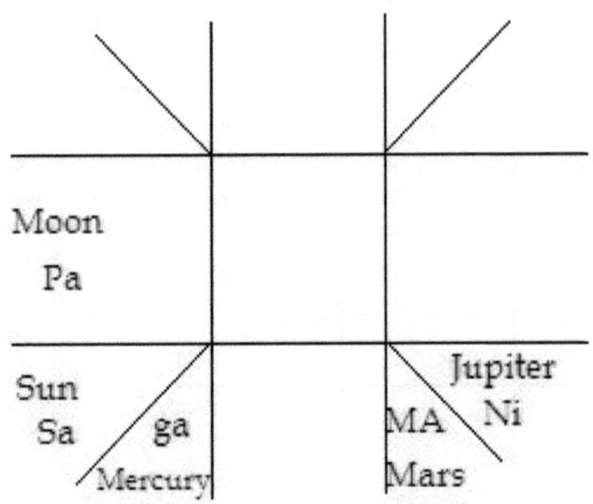


*Planetary position of Multani's Arohan*

As in the raga Todi, the emotions are like the melancholy of impersonality. But on the other hand, the emotions of the raga Multani are exhaustion, fatigue, and melancholy. Universal poet Rabindranath Tagore said, "*Multan is like the tired breathing of the end of a fervent sunny day.*" ('Sangeeter Mukti', "Sangeet Chinta")

The Vadi swar of raga Multani is Pa, and the Samvadi swar is Sa. That means the Moon and the Sun are the main ruler planets of this raga. At the time of Arohon, it excluded the Komal re and Komal dha, which means, as per our consideration, the emotion of this raga is developed without faith, devotion and cordiality. But at the time of descending, it includes Komal re and Komal dha. So we can say that at the time of Abarohan, the tunes of this raga, we feel the emotion of faith, devotion, and heartiness. But, on the other hand, this vacillating movement of re, dha incites or inspires emotions like the depression of exhaustion and weariness.

V

We have placed the examples of those ragas whose *Vadi* swar and *Samvadi* swar are different. Now we want to discuss that kind of ragas whose *Vadi* and *Samvadi* swars are the same, but the emotions, nature, and sentiments are different.

We can consider raga Lalit and raga Malkauns. The *Vadi* swar of these two ragas is Ma (*suddha madhyam*), and the *Samvadi* swar is Sa (Sadoj). But emotion, nature, and sentiments are different.

**Lalit:** The nature of Lalit is apathetic solemnity. The permanent sentiment is *shringar* (full of desire). But there is some dissatisfaction in that shringar-sentiment. As per our consideration, the leading cause of that dissatisfaction is only the absence of *pancham* (Pa), the Moon. In this raga, two *madhyams* (Ma & MA) are used.

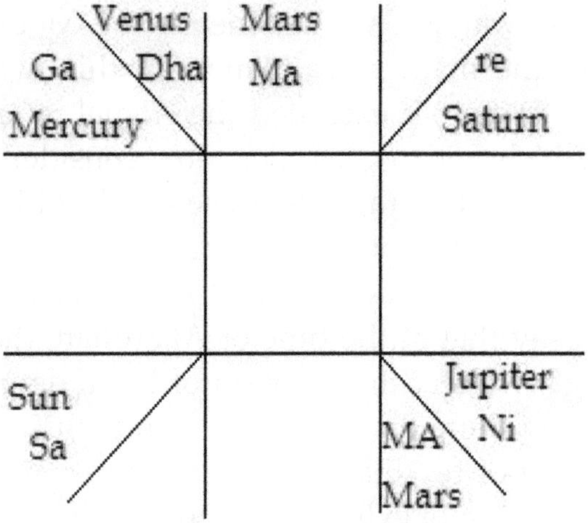

Venus
Ga Dha
Mercury
Mars
Ma
re
Saturn
Sun
Sa
Jupiter
MA Ni
Mars

*Planetary position of Raga Lalit*

As per the version of poet Kazi Nazrul Islam, "*Lalit has no leg; he is swinging in the lap of two mothers in the morning.*" [In the Bengali vocabulary, '*Pa*' means leg, and '*Ma*' means the mother. So the poet mockingly said that Lalit has two mothers and has no legs.] And the *Komal* re of this raga influenced by Saturn brings apathy. The ni (*Komal nishad*) means the Jupiter of Pisces brings an incomparable depth of emotion. And the *Pakad* like MA Dha MA Ma or Ga Ma MA Ga MA Dha brings the emotion of *shringer* (desire), but as the presence of MA in *Pakad*, thefeeling of dissatisfaction comes with that emotion of *shringer*. And the oscillation of this dissatisfaction and *shringer* brings its permanent emotion as an apathetic solemnity.

**Malkauns:** On the other hand, *Tibra madhyam* (MA) is absent in raga Malkauns. So there are no dissatisfactory or oscillatory feelings. This raga is free from the influence of the Moon and Saturn. Because Pa and Re swars are not used here, for this reason, the feeling of this raga is free from restlessness and decomposition of tiredness and brings the permanent emotion of *Shanta* (peace) and seriousness.

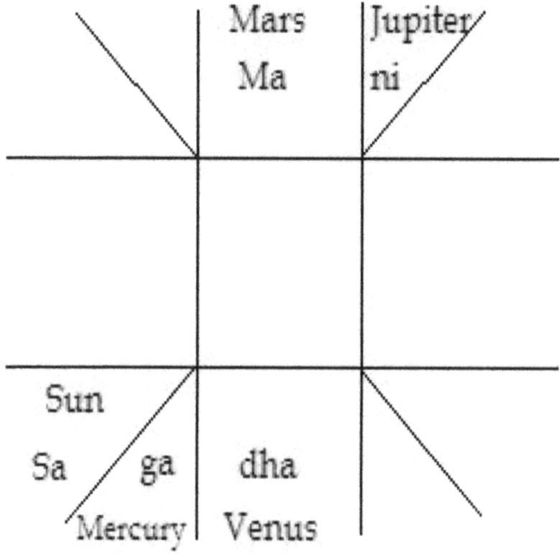


*Planetary position of Raga Malkauns*

**Basant:** Likewise, the *Vadi* and the *Samvadi* swars of raga Basant are Sa' (Sadoj of *taar saptak*—the highest range of the three registers) and Pa. The swars like re, dha, Ma, and MA are used in this raga.

The *Pakar* (*Pakad*) is MA Ga Ma Ga re Sa of raga Basant. At the time of *Arohon*, the swars ascend as Sa Ga MA dha Re' Sa', and *Abarohon* order is Sa' Ni, dha, Pa, MA Ga MA Ga Re Sa. The notable matter is the absence of the Pa and Ni, which means the absence of the Moon and Jupiter. These two planets are the controller of the emotions of the mind and religious feelings, respectively.

In the absence of these two swars as well as two planets, those emotions are weak in the raga Basant. And the repeated presence of Ga MA swars brings emotions like indecisiveness, restless joy and sober

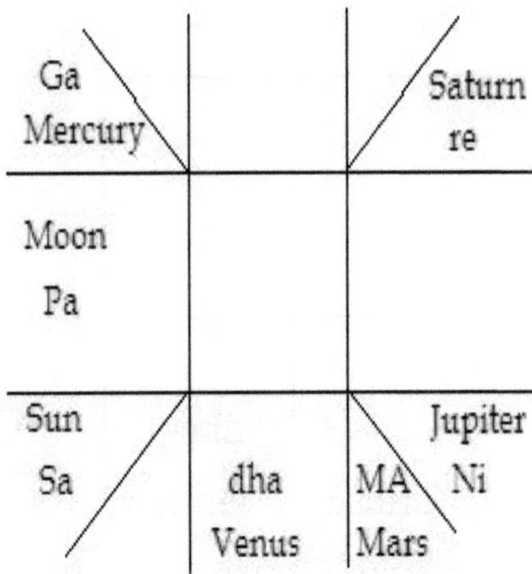


*Planetary position of Raga Basant*

solemnity. This combination of emotions brings the feelings of spring.

**Paroj:** In Paroj, the *Vadi* swar is Sa (the Sadoj of *madhya saptak* – the basic gamut range of the three *saptak*), and the *Samvadi* swar is Pa. And re, dha, Ma and MA swars are also used in this raga. The *Pakar* (or *Pakad*) are Sa' Ni dha Pa MA Pa, Ga Ma Pa of the Paroj.

The main chain of raga Paroj is MA, dha, re Sa, re Ni dha Pa. *Arohon* of Paroj is Ni Sa Ga MA dha Ni Sa' (Ni denotes the nishad of *mandra saptak*— the first or lower range of the three *saptak*) and *Abahoron* is Sa' Ni dha Pa, Ga Ma Ga, MA Ga Re Sa.

The notable matter is the absence of Re at the time of *arohon*. And re and dha is *Komal*, and there is the presence of two madhyams (Ma & MA). The Ni swar

| | | |
|---|---|---|
| Ga<br>Mercury | Ma<br>Mars | re<br>Saturn |
| Moon<br>Pa | | |
| Sun<br>Sa | dha<br>Venus | Jupiter<br>MA Ni<br>Mars |

*Planetary position of Raga Paroj*

gets special importance in this raga. Pa uttered as the giver of pleasure. That is due to the special significance of Pa and Ni, the Moon and Jupiter. It brings the feeling of grief with the restless emotion of spring. Although the two ragas (Basant & Paroj) are similar in listening, the emotions of these two are different. The cause of the different emotions is only the placement of swars, the chain of swars, and the influence of planets accordingly. The main difference between these two ragas is that in Basant, there is a sense of restrained emotion, while in Paroj, the emotion manifests with that emotion.

**Ashavori:** The *Vadi* swar of Ashavori is Dha, and the *Sambadhi* swar is Ga. That means the *Vadi* swar Dha is influenced by Venus or Love. And *Samvadi* swar Ga is influenced by Mercury which gives analysis, criticism, presence of mind, rationality, patience, intelligence, etc. Only ga, dha, and ni are *Komal* (flat), and the other swars are *Suddha* (natural).

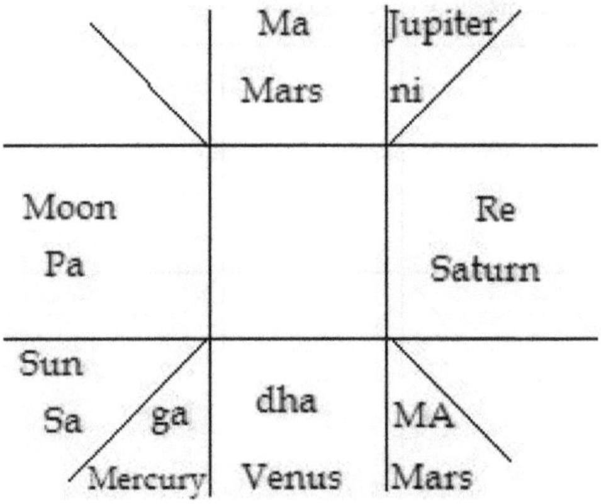

Ma
Mars
Jupiter
ni
Moon
Pa
Re
Saturn
Sun
Sa
ga
Mercury
dha
Venus
MA
Mars

*Planetary position of Raga Ashavori*

At the time of the *Arohan*, it goes without Ga and Ni. That means this raga avoids the feelings of spiritualism at its ascending time. The madhyam (Ma) of this raga is weak. So, the emotion of willpower is weak. At the time of the movement of the tune, Ga creates harmony with Pa, which means it establishes harmony with Mercury and the Moon. As per the astrological view, raga Ashavori moves with sense, intelligence, and mind coherence. Its nature is calm due to the harmony of sense and mind.

**Jainpuri:** Like raga Ashavori, we find another raga named Jainpuri. The *Vadi* swar of Jainpuri is Ni, *Samvadi* swar is Dha. And the swar Ga is absent at the time of ascending. But due to the influence of Ni, the Jupiter, the nature of this raga is serious.

VI

We can write down more and more examples. But it should not be necessary just now. We tried to explain that the seven planets influence twelve swars of Indian music. Each raga's different emotions rise only because of the importance and sequence of swars. For the same reason, it creates several emotional effects on the human mind. As a cause of planetary influence, the tunes of music act on every animal. In this connection, we can also do music therapy through astrology. The astrologers can advise their clients to listen to a raga or song, as they suggest the precious gemstone to any person as a remedial measure by examining the querent's birth chart (horoscope). If the astrologer finds the Sun is weak in the horoscope, he can advise his client to listen to those ragas, tunes, or songs whose *Vadi* swar is Sa (Sadoj). If he thinks to give power to the Venus of his querent, he can advise listening to the tunes whose *Vadi* swar is Dha. And in this way, music therapy can be applied through astrological examination.

# Plametary Roles in Musical Scales

We have talked about the planetary influence over musical swars in the previous chapter. Now we talk about the planetary influence over musical scale and chord. It is essential to select the perfect scale and/or chord before singing or playing the music and treat patients through music therapy.

So, first, let's talk about musical scale selection. We know that every musician sings and plays on a particular scale. This scale is significant to musicians and music students. Scale means to play or sing a specific tune with the swar 'Sa'. If the scale selection is inappropriate, the song and melody of the singer's music may significantly reduce. Or may not expose or organise properly. Unfortunately, we could not get the proper answer to why this happened.

In the case of many artists, it has been found that they may have sung the same song; one's song was very well accepted by the audience, while another's song did not well. For example, *Shyama sangeet* has been expressed beautifully in the voice of Pannalal Bhattacharya, as it has not been expressed so appreciating in the voice of any other. On the other hand, singer and composer Hemanta Mukhopadhyay or Shyamal Mitra's romantic songs could not come out as many different singers did. One of the reasons is the sweetness of their voice, and another is the selection of the appropriate scale.

We do not say that great musicians didn't understand the scale of their music. But before singing, the choice of the scale by some significant musicians may not match their zodiac sign. In the present discussion, we would like to discuss this matter. But, before that, we need to know the scale of music.

A musical scale is a set of notes in a simple rhythmic tempo. There is a harmony of the melody between these positions, creating a balance of the frequency of the tune. For instance, we like the music of drumbeats during Durga Puja. But if an incompetent person beats the drum, it becomes inaudible and unbearable. Because the expert hand of the drummer hits the drum with various rhythms and creates impressive, pleasant harmony, an inexpert and off-key person cannot make that. This harmony is essential in tune and rhythm. Experienced musicians can create many variations with the help of different intersections and breaks.

As we know, the seven swars in Indian Music are Sa, Re, Ga, Ma, Pa, Dha and Ni; they are referred to by the notes like C, D, E, F, G, A and B, respectively, in the Western tradition. And "flat" and "sharp" terms of western music are known as "*Komal*" and "*Tibra*" swars, respectively, in Indian Music. According to the West, any musical instrument's positions of tones are fixed in a specific mathematical gap. For example, after tying a thread or string from one end to the other and is divided into 53 equal parts, the vibration of the tones C, D, E, F, G, A and B can be found if it struck at the head on 9-8-5-9-8-9-5th division. But the swars of Indian music do not have this specific mathematical position. Instead, it depends upon *Shruti* (the pleasant musical sounds and a particular division of *Saptak* (octave)). According to musicology, seven swars built-in from twenty-two Shrutis. This *Shruti* depends upon the sense of hearing. As a result, the instrument's notes position entirely depends upon the hearing ability of the person preparing the musical instrument. Again, in the case of Western notes, the preceding and following swars (notes) are marked as flat and sharp, respectively. As a result, each swar from Sa to Ni has *bikrito* swar, i.e. flat and/or sharp. But in Indian music, five swars are identified as *bikrito* swars, taking re ga dha ni as only *Komal* (flat) and MA as *Tibra* (sharp).

The musician takes any of the seven swars and the five *bikrito* swars as the starting note of the musical performance per his wish or ability. That initial swar refers to the Western note (swar). For example, if the singer performs music with the initial note "Sa" as the position of G# of Western tone, then his scale would be called "G Sharp". So if a musician starts or sets Sa in B flat, then the scale will be called "B flat". Similarly, the scale is known by different names like "Natural A", "Natural C", "F sharp", etc. In Indian musical terms, this method is called "changing the *Kharaj*". That is to change the position of Sadoj (Sa). As it commonly said, "Singing as setting Sadoj (Sa) to suddha madhyam (Ma)" or "setting Sa to *suddha Gandhar* (Ga)", etc.

Another term for western music is the chord. The position of the first-third-fifth tone is called a chord. This chord can be of several types, like major, minor, harmonic, pentatonic etc. This arrangement of first-third-fifth notes is called the major scale, like Sa-Ga-Pa (C-E-G). Again Sa-ga (Komal Gandhar)-Pa (C-E*b*-G). This chain is called the minor scale. Such groupings of swars are called chords in Western terms. This chord depends on the significant tone the artist will be performing the music. Simply put, a scale is a series of successively placed or accented swars. And chords are groups of swars that are pronounced or voiced together.

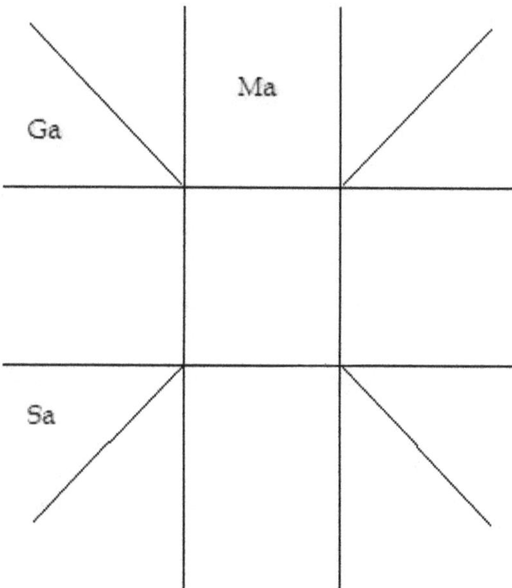


*Planetary position of Mejor Scale*

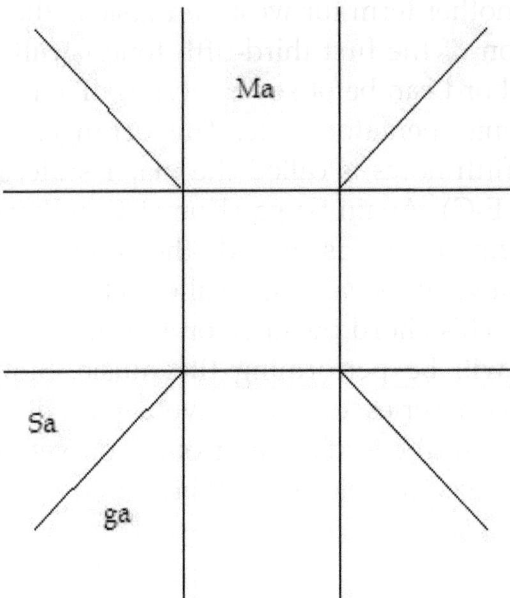


*Planetary position of Minor Scale*

II

Now it is necessary to judge which tone the artist will adopt and choose his scale and major chords. If a musician is an Aries ascendant or Aries sign person, then *Shuddha Gandhar* is in the third, i.e, house of the courage of his zodiac sign. Because the third house of the Aries signs, there is Gemini. And the ruler of Gemini is *Gandhar*. And the fourth house of Aries, i.e, Cancer. The Moon is the ruler of Cancer, and Moon is the lord of the swar *Pancham* (Pa). And in fifth place is *Sadaj* or Sa. Because Sa is influenced by the Sun, and Sun is the ruler of Leo, which is situated in fifth position from the Aries. So, it will be good if the artist sings with a major scale. But if an Aries person chooses a minor scale, the scale may not be suitable for that artist because of the presence of *Komal Gandhar* (ga). This ga, as per our consideration, is placed in Virgo in the 6th house from the Aries sign. And as per astrological consideration, Virgo is the enemy field of Aries. So if an Aries artist performs music on a minor scale, its impact on the public may be temporary or adverse. In the case of such a Cancer Musician, the minor scale could be as helpful in developing his talent as the major scale will not be because the middle swar of the major scale is suddha Gandhar (Ga), the lord of the twelfth house and the lord of expenditure of Cancer signs.

God blesses Taurus and Gemini musicians. They can sing in any major or minor scale or chord or, in some cases, both chords and/or scales. On both scales, they can capture the attention of the audience.

# The Taste in Music

Indian music is capable of curing many human ailments. Just as the flow of music or the rhythm can bring about specific changes in the human mind, the release of hormones and the function of the glands may go appropriately by the touch of tune. It controls some infections, secretion of various glands, blood pressure etc. Some music therapists say that Ahir Bhairava Raga can improve digestion or remedy indigestion, heartburn, or acidity. The Ashabari raga helps to boost confidence, Bageshree raga is especially useful for insomnia. Basanta bahar raga helps treat gallstones, Bhairavi raga works well for rheumatic arthritis, Bhimpalashree relieves anxiety or worry, Chandrakosha cures anorexia etc. So we have an extensive list of those ragas with which various diseases can be alleviated/cured. Or the secretion of any fluid or chemical synthesis may help to balance favourable and unfavourable conditions.

Although experienced music therapists have given such long lists, we disagree with their thinking. Because we know that, as per allopathy medicine, paracetamol can reduce the patient's body temperature, and telmisartan, amlodipine, and cilnidipine, help control blood pressure. Although these medicines can be used by everyone, experienced doctors do not prescribe these kinds of medicament indiscriminately to any patient. After understanding the patient's symptoms, telmisartan, amlodipine or chlorthalidone, hydrochlorothiazide etc., whichever is necessary, can be given. Selecting medicine to cure the disease is important for the patient. After using that infallible medicine, the patient recovered. However, it has also been observed that the same medication and treatment sometimes do not work for all. Instead of relief, it increases the risk of someone's disease. The truth is that every person's constitution is different. So all medicines do not work equally in everyone's body. So that doctors try to know a patient's physical and mental condition before treatment. Especially before homoeopathy treatment, doctors ask various questions to the patient and the people of the patient's house, after knowing all information and then prescribing the medicine. Just as doctors choose medicine by judging the patient's physical and mental constitution, in music therapy, the therapist should choose the melody or raga of the music according to the patient's mental status. Because we cannot insist that everyone will like the same types of songs or can use the same song to cure the same disease, so we think that we should first understand the taste in the music of each patient, then should suggest which genre of tune or which raga can cure the particular disease of the patient. If the music, song, raga or rhythm is against the patient's taste, it will not cure the disease but cause harm. Therefore, it should be necessary to determine the musical taste based on the patient's zodiac.

Treatment through music, therefore, requires identifying the patient's taste in music. If treated according to taste, through the rhythm or the tune, the work of healing or relief will be easy. Otherwise, if you apply it like a blind person knowing that such raga, such rhythm, such a melody can cure such a disease, it will not cure the disease; On the other hand, there may be an increase of the severity, hazards and problems of the illness or there will be the risk of the worst. That's why if you want to heal any patient through music, first, it is necessary to know the patient's taste in music, i.e. what kind of music, melody or rhythm the patient likes. Otherwise, a person who likes mellow songs or worship music will not be touched or given any joy by listening to pop music or mass music. The tune of such a contrary taste will never be able to cure the disease. So, before the music therapy, we should understand the patient's taste in music.

Nine rasas (the rasas are the sentiment or emotion evoked in every person by the art) are active in Indian music. The flow of this rasas felt in the mind of every socialite human being. But there is some variation in that feeling. Different people have different sentiments or tastes is the main reason. Some people like only comedy songs, some people like tragedy, and others like to be overwhelmed with devotion. In the case of music, too, some people like devotional songs, some people like mass songs, and some people like patriotic songs or war songs. Someone is a fan of romantic songs. Some people like serious songs. The reason for such different preferences is the basic chemistry of the listener's mind. That's the main cause of the taste.

Now let's have a couple of discussions about people's music taste through Indian astrology.

II

Musicologists say nine *rasas* are active in Indian music. The flow of those nine *rasas* can be felt by every social in their mind. But there is some variation in that feeling. The variety of the main *rasa* of different people is the main reason for that feeling of variation. The type of people's tastes also depends on the planetary position in their horoscope, especially from the nature of their birth sign.

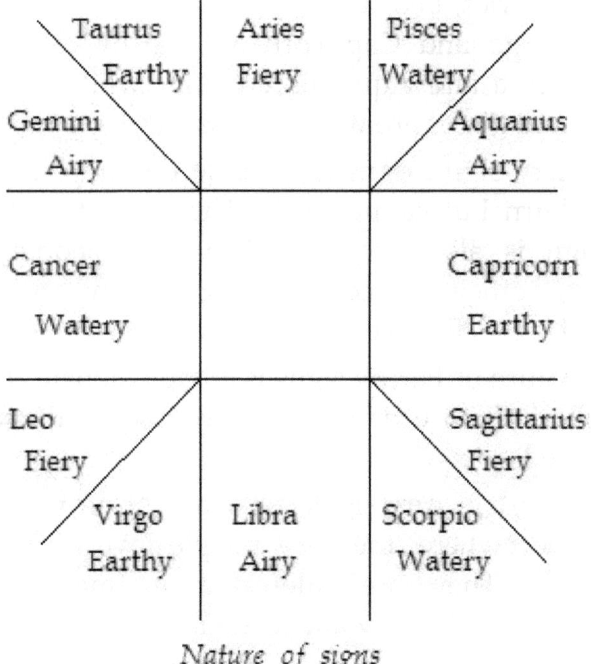


*Nature of signs*

According to Indian astrology, the twelve zodiac signs divide into four natures: Fiery, Earthy, Airy, and Watery. As a result, a person of any zodiac sign is born with the usual mental nature. As we see, some people are courageous, and some people are very compassionate. Some people are very light-hearted. Some people are very serious-minded. One of the reasons for this nature is the influence of the principal character of his birth sign. The nature of *Atmakaraka* planets can also be one of the reasons for this. The *Atmakaraka* planet is the principal or main significator among seven planets, with maximum degrees in any sign. It means the significator of the self.

Now let us talk about these four natures of Fiery-Earthy-Airy-Watery signs. According to the scriptures, Aries, Leo, and Sagittarius are Fiery signs. Taurus, Virgo and Capricorn are Earthy elements. Gemini, Libra and Aquarius are Airy while Cancer, Scorpio, and Pisces are watery signs.

The fiery sign means fiery. Like the fire can only execute burn but cannot wait. The character of the fiery sign is also like that. The fiery people are dynamic, efficient, coordinating when needed, powerful, agile, flexible, precise, and refined.

The nature of Earthy signs is compassionate. They don't like influence or violence. By nature, they are soft-hearted.

The nature of Airy signs is like air. As air wants to spread everywhere, the Airy people love to extend themselves. They are interested in maintaining communication. They want to establish a fresh style by removing old ideas, like the fresh air displacing the stale air.

The nature of watery signs is artistic, romantic and creative.

These four types of signs are associated with the three natures or levels in the zodiac. Those levels are moveable, fixed, and mutable/dual.

| | | |
|---|---|---|
| Taurus Earthy Fixed<br>Airy Dual Gemini | Aries<br>Fiery<br>Moveable | Pisces Watery Dual<br>Fixed Airy Aquarius |
| Cancer<br>Moveable<br>Watery | | Capricorn<br>Moveable<br>Earthy |
| Leo Fixed Fiery<br>Virgo Dual Earthy | Libra<br>Moveable<br>Airy | Sagittarius Fiery Dual<br>Fixed Scorpio Watery |

*Nature of signs*

The nature of moveable signs is fickleness and dynamism. It governs the motion of the human mind of this nature and initiates the workforce—the essential elements like enthusiasm, enthusiasm, primary research, activity, restlessness, versatility etc.

The nature of fixed signs indicates constancy, equanimity, and patience are the principal features of its nature. As a result, this class of people has qualities such as seriousness, importance, self-centeredness, concentration, discipline, perseverance, endurance, hard work, etc.

The nature of mutable/dual signs have mixed elements of moveable and fixed signs. Its nature manifests itself by combining the nature of the moveable and fixed signs. For example, when outside is joyful, inside is serious; Inwardly self-centred, outwardly full of festivities; Outside is fast, inside is slow, steady.

The essential nature of the human character is created by mixing these three principal natures with the four instincts. Accordingly, the levels or classes are moveable-fiery, moveable-earthy, moveable-airy, and moveable-watery. For example, Aries, Capricorn, Libra, and Cancer.

Fixed-fiery, fixed-earthy, fixed-airy, fixed-watery. For instance, Leo, Taurus, Aquarius, and Scorpio.

Dual-fiery, dual-earthy, dual-airy, dual-watery. For example, Sagittarius, Virgo, Gemini, and Pisces.

The fundamental nature of Movable-Fiery signs is a combination of movable and fiery instincts. They are fickle, dynamic, active, coordinated when necessary, heroic, agile, flexible, transparent, and prudent. In addition, essential elements connect enthusiasm, primary research, performance, multi-variability, etc. This nature is found in the Aries signs.

The fundamental nature of moveable- Earthy signs is compassion. They don't like influence or violence. Characteristically they are soft-minded, fickle, and dynamic. They coordinate when necessary. They are heroic, agile, flexible, transparent, and prudent. In addition, they coordinate as needed. They are enthusiastic. Primary research, performance, and multi-variability compassion are their essential elements. This combination of nature is found in the Capricorn sign.

And the nature of moveable-airy, moveable-watery and other signs are a combination of moveable and airy, moveable and watery characters and so on.

The nature of moveable-airy signs builds by combining moveable and airy personalities. Airy characters are just like air. They love to expand themselves. They are interested in maintaining communication and want to establish a fresh style by removing old ideas, like the fresh air displacing the stale air. And these characteristic relate to the nature of moveable signs like fickleness and dynamism. It governs the motion of the human mind of this nature and initiates the workforce—the essential elements like enthusiasm, primary research, activity, restlessness, versatility etc. This combination of nature can be found in the Libra Sign.

The nature of the moveable-watery sign is an amalgamation of watery and moveable characters. As watery signs, their mentality grows artistic and romantic, and like water current, they are fickle, deep, severe yet romantic, creative and sometimes destructive. And this attributes the character of moveable signs like fickleness and dynamism. It governs the motion of the human mind of this nature and initiates the workforce—the essential elements like enthusiasm, primary research, activity, restlessness, versatility etc., are connected. We can find this combination of nature in the Cancer sign.

The nature of fixed-fiery signs combines fiery and fixed characters. As per fiery, they are fickle, dynamic, active. They coordinate when necessary. They are heroic, agile, flexible, transparent, and prudent. With these attributes, the character of fixed signs like constancy, equanimity and patience, seriousness, importance, self-centeredness, concentration, discipline, perseverance, endurance, hard work etc., are connected. We can find this combination of nature in the people of Leo sign.

The nature of fixed-earthy signs is the combination of earthy and fixed character. So as per earthy signs, they don't like violence. Their characteristics are soft-mindedness and fickleness. They are dynamic and show more coordination when necessary. They are heroic, agility, flexibility, transparency, and prudence. In addition, constancy, equanimity and patience, seriousness, importance, self-centeredness, concentration, discipline, perseverance, endurance, hard work etc., are connected to their nature. The fundamental nature of Taurus signs is like this.

The nature of fixed-airy signs is the combination of airy and fixed characters. The airy means they love to spread themselves everywhere. They are interested in maintaining communication. They want to establish a new style by removing old ideas like stale air and bringing in fresh air. And these characteristics relate to fixed sign's nature, like constancy, equanimity and patience, seriousness, importance, self-centeredness, concentration, discipline, perseverance, endurance, hard work etc. The nature of Aquarius sings full of these attributes.

The nature of fixed-watery signs combines watery and fixed characters. As watery signs, their mentality grows artistic and romantic, and like water current, they are fickle, deep, severe yet romantic, creative and sometimes destructive. And these attributes, the character of moveable signs like constancy, equanimity and patience, seriousness, importance, self-centeredness, concentration, discipline, perseverance, endurance, hard work etc., are connected. We can find these attributes in Scorpio signs.

The nature of dual-fiery signs is the combination of fiery and dual characters. As per fiery, they are fickle, dynamic, active, coordinated when necessary, heroic, agile, flexible, transparent, and prudent. With these attributes, the character of dual signs. The nature of dual signs manifests by combining the nature of the moveable and fixed signs. When outside is joyful, inside is serious; inwardly self-centred, outwardly full of festivities; Outside is fast; inside is slow, steady. This combination of nature is found in Sagittarius signs.

The nature of dual-earthy signs is the combination of earthy and dual characters. So as per earthy signs, they don't like violence. Their characteristics are soft-mindedness and fickleness, dynamic, more coordination when necessary, heroic, agility, flexibility, transparency, and prudence. The nature of dual signs manifests by combining the nature of the moveable and fixed signs. So when outside is joyful, inside is serious; inwardly self-centred, outwardly full of festivities; Outside is fast; inside is slow, steady. This combination of nature is found in Virgo signs.

The nature of dual-airy signs is the combination of airy and dual characters. The airy means they love to spread themselves everywhere. They are interested in maintaining communication. They want to establish a new style by removing old ideas like stale air and bringing in fresh air. And these characteristic relate to the nature of dual signs—that mixture of two seemingly opposite characters, fixed and moveable natures. So when outside is joyful, inside is serious; inwardly self-centred, outwardly full of festivities; Outside is fast; inside is slow, steady. This combination of nature is found in Gemini signs.

The nature of dual-watery signs combines watery and dual characters. As watery signs, their mentality grows artistic and romantic, and like water current, they are fickle, deep, severe yet romantic, creative and sometimes destructive. The nature of dual signs manifests by combining the nature of the moveable and fixed signs. So when outside is joyful, inside is serious; inwardly self-centred, outwardly full of festivities; Outside is fast; inside is slow, steady. This combination of nature is found in Pisces signs.

III

After knowing the nature of signs, we should give special attention to the patient's *Atmakaraka-planet*. The *Atmakaraka-planet* is the principal or main significator among seven planets, with maximum degrees in any sign. It means the significator of the self. The patient's taste depends a lot on the

*Atmakaraka-planet*. If the *Atmakarak-planet* of a patient is the sun, then his favourite music may be fast rhythmic songs. But that song should also be interesting.

On the other hand, if *Atmakaraka-planet* is the moon, he will like romantic songs, especially songs that express great beauty. If *Atmakaraka-planet* is Mars, it should understand that the native may have a fighting spirit. So he may prefer war music, folk music, patriotic music, pop, rock songs or upbeat music with movement. But, on the other hand, if *Atmakaraka* is Mercury, the native will like classical songs, raga music, or any songs that contain knowledge or some deep or heavy theory.

Whose *Atmakaraka-planet* is Jupiter, they usually prefer calm, melodic, devotional songs, songs with a quiet mood, light-hearted kirtan songs, spiritual songs etc. etc. The person whose *Atmakaraka-planet* is Venus will love romantic songs, and any tender music or romanticism in nature will love this expressive song, worship music or expressive songs with romanticism. On the other hand, if Saturn is the *Atmakaraka-planet*, they will like spiritual songs, loud kirtans, and mind-blowing music, sad songs.

IV

Now let's give examples of some famous Indian musicians. From that illustration, the reader can easily understand our formulas. For instance, we want to mention the names of many artists, but it is not possible due to the artists' lack of accurate birth details of artists. Moreover, the difference in date of birth and time of some renowned artists and their zodiac signs has obstructed our research.

Dhananjay Bhattacharya (10 September 1922), Sign is Aries. That means Fiery sign. According to our consideration, his nature was active, dynamic, functional, coordinating when necessary, and vigorous with fundamental elements like enthusiasm, originality, research, activity, versatility etc. Also flexible and precise, refined personality.

When we recall Dhananjaya Bhattacharya's patriotic, romantic, devotional songs, we see his enthusiastic, exuberant, romantic personality. Aries people's musical taste is like Dhananjaya Bhattacharya.

Singer Asha Bhosle (8 September 1933) Aries. Another famous singer Manna Dey (1 May 1919), was also an Aries. However, according to another source, Manna Dey was Taurus. The only reason for this difference is the non-availability of accurate birth time information.

Hemanta Mukhopadhyay (16 June 1920) was a Taurus. That is a fixed-earthy sign. According to the sources, his nature includes seriousness, self-centeredness, concentration, discipline, perseverance, tolerance, hard work etc. Also, he didn't like aggressiveness due to his natural instinct. If we think about Hemanta Mukhopadhyay's songs, we can see that he never sang songs of extreme madness. Even if he did, the audience did not take particular care of that song. There was seriousness and romanticism in his songs. Based on his illustration, Taurus listeners do not like aggressive songs.

Now, if someone asks, can any Taurus man sing like Hemanta Mukherjee? We will say 'No' to his answer because tastes in music and singing are different. Taste in music may include song selection and choice, but when it comes to singing, the second house, i.e. voice, and the fifth house, i.e. talent, should be judged carefully. But we are not going that way for now. We are here to talk about the types of music liked by specific types of people.

Sandhya Mukhopadhyay (4 October 1931), Gemini. i.e., dual-airy sign. According to our sources, the main characteristic of this zodiac sign is that they are interested in maintaining communication. They are interested in breaking old ideas and establishing new trends like fresh air. When outwardly is fickle, then inwardly is serious. When inwardly self-centred, then outwardly full of festivities; when outwardly fast, inwardly slow, steady.

Singer Manabendra Mukherjee (11 August 1931, Gemini) also possesses this temperament and musical taste.

Lata Mangeshkar (28 September 1929), Cancer sign. i.e., moveable-watery sign. In our view, her characteristic is like water currents, fickle, deep, severe yet romantic, creative, and sometimes destructive. However, this destruction does not mean waste; the annihilation of the old for the creation of the new. And enthusiasm, activity, Variability, restlessness, etc., have mixed with those qualities. Therefore, one can find a gathering of solemn yet romantic expressions with diversity in her songs. And at the same time, there is enthusiasm to do something new.

On the other hand, she is devoted to the old style and has the trend and attraction to create the modern style. According to sources, we think that the music taste of Cancer people is as varied as that of Lata Mangeshkar. Sometimes it is old traditional, occasionally new trends oriented. Another legendary singer Kishore Kumar (4 August 1929), was also a Cancer sign.

Singer and composer Shyamal Mitra (born on 14 January 1929) was born in the Aquarius sign. i.e., fixed-airy signs. According to the sources, the qualities of seriousness, self-centeredness, concentration, discipline, perseverance, endurance, hard work etc., existed in his nature. At the same time, he tried to establish a fresh style by removing the old style. Renowned composer and singer Sachin Dev Burman (1 October 1906) was also an Aquarius. His contribution to popularising Bengali folk music is undeniable.

Renowned Rabindra Sangeet singer Kanika Bandyopadhyay (12 October 1924) was a Pisces. According to our consideration, Pisces is a mutable-watery sign. The nature of Pisces is artistic, romantic and creative. Characteristics consist of mixed elements of moveable and fixed signs. It manifests itself in the combination of moveable and static nature. When outside is joyful, inside is serious. When inwardly self-centred, then outwardly affable and full of festivities. But, while the outwardly is dynamic, the inwardly is slow and steady. The truth of these words can only be understood by listening to Kanika Banerjee's excellent soulful songs. When she performs, her melody is dynamic, and then inwardly, she is calm and quiet. Pisces people's taste in music is similar to Kanika Banerjee's musical taste.

V

According to the similarities and differences, the twelve signs in the zodiac can observe the musical tastes of the people of the twelve signs. By this formula, it is possible to find the musical taste of any person. Therefore, even looking at each person's horoscope, we can predict what kind of music they might be treated to and indicate which genre of music an artist can gain fame.

In the above example, Sandhya Mukherjee and Manabendra Mukherjee were Gemini signs. According to our sources, the tastes of the two were similar. But there is some difference in their performance because of singing style, vocal richness, tone projection etc., due to the position of the second house and its lord from their Lagna (ascendant) in their birth chart.

According to Astrology, knowing people's musical tastes is vital before music therapy. It will not be easy to accept the music if the patient doesn't like it. In addition, disliked music may aggravate the disease rather than cure it by making the patient intolerable. So knowing the patient's taste in music is the first imperative for music therapy.

# Disease according to Astrology

If a person has a disease, they must go to a doctor. If there is no disease, no doctor can treat the patient. But, again, doctors cannot answer when or how long a patient may suffer if he gets sick because doctors search for diseases by looking at physical symptoms. The duration of the patient's recovery is estimated by looking at the patient's condition after administering the medicine.

On the other hand, before a disease occurs, astrology can assume when and how long a person may suffer from a disease, even which disease may turn into a chronic illness, in which disease the person will continue to suffer from temporary problems.

Whether a medical failure or doctor's dilemma will happen or not, even if a person is a disease-luxurious attitude, all can easily find out through astrological calculation and prediction.

It can also say that the doctor of which race, like Brahmin, Kshatriya, Vaishya, Shudra, Mlechcha, restless nature, hairless, calm, short-tempered, boyish nature etc., may be able to cure the disease of the particular patient. That is because, as per astrology scripture belief, human diseases and cures depend on the position of the planets.

Let's briefly discuss how we can diagnose diseases according to astrology. If any reader is particularly interested in this subject, he should properly study '*Rogadhya*' (the chapter contains 'determination of disease') of Astrology. Here only the methods of diagnosis are discussed in a few words. Because we want to say- music can be used to cure people's diseases, which we named 'music therapy'. But, according to Astrology, firstly, one must know about the person's disease to treat by music. That is why we want to discuss the diagnosis briefly in the present chapter.

II

To determine the disease of any human being, one has first to consider the *dhat* or *tridosha* of the patient, which means whether he is Vayu/Vata (Air), Pitta (Bile) & Kapha (Phlegm) or mixed *dhat*.

So firstly, one must know the person's nature, i.e., whether he is Vayu-Pitta-Kapha (Air-Bile-Phlegm) or mixed dhats. What we call dhat in ordinary language, in Ayurvedic terms, is called '*dosha*'—doshas are of three types and hence called—'*tridoshas*'. These are the elemental physical energies and govern essential factors of the body's entire physical structure and functions. The easy way to know this *dosha* or *dhat* is to judge on which planet the person was born or which is the *Atmakarak* (the strongest influenced) planet of the native.

Among the planets, the Sun and Mars are of Pitta (bile) dhat, Moon and Venus are of Kapha (phlegm), Saturn is Vayu (air), and the dhat of Mercury and Jupiter are of mixed, i.e. Pitta and Kapha combined, but the body is of Vayu (air). On the other hand, the dhat of Jupiter is Kapha, Saturn, Rahu, and Ketu are Vayu (air), and the dhat of Venus is Kapha, but the body is Vayu.

Among the twelve zodiac signs, the dhat of Aries is Pitta (bile), Taurus is Vayu (air), Gemini is mixed (combined), Cancer is Kapha (phlegm), Leo is Pitta, dhat of Virgo is Vayu, Libra is mixed, Scorpio is Kapha, Sagittarius is Pitta, Capricorn is Vayu, Aquarius Mixed, and Pisces is Kapha by dhat. Let's draw a table–

| Nature | Dhat | Rashi | | |
|---|---|---|---|---|
| Firey | Pitta | Aries | Leo | Sagittarius |
| Earthy | Vayu | Taurus | Virgo | Capricorn |
| Airy | Mixed | Gemini | Libra | Aquarius |
| Watery | Kapha | Cancer | Scorpio | Pisces |

*Nature & Dhat of Signs*

III

The twelve zodiac signs identify the twelve parts of the human body, such as Aries head, Taurus face, Gemini arms, Cancer heart, Leo belly, Virgo lower back, Libra lower abdomen (below the navel), Scorpio anus, Capricorn genitals and Pisces two feet.

Nine planets are considered the rulers of nine dhatus. For example, the Sun is the ruler of bones, Moon is the ruler of blood, Mars is of marrow and blood, Mercury is the ruler of skin (thin skin), Jupiter is of skin, Venus is of semen, and Saturn is the ruler of the Nadi (the artery and veins). Rahu is the ruler of eruptions, tumours, bone joint problems, acne etc., and Ketu is the ruler of skin diseases, colic, sores, ulcers, rotten sores etc.

If an astrologer wants to know about the disease of a particular person, first, he must judge the patient's zodiac sign. Twelve houses of the zodiac consider body parts. According to Jyotish, Lagna considers the first house, second, third, fourth, fifth, sixth etc. so on, up to the twelfth house, to calculate to diagnose the disease. The brain or head of the native is to be judged from the first house. Similarly, eyes, mouth, throat, tongue, face etc., are considered from the second house. Two arms, neck, and ears are judged from the third house. From the fourth house, lungs, chest, heart, etc. are judged; stomach and

| | | |
|---|---|---|
| Taurus 2nd<br>Gemini 3rd | Aries<br>Ascendant<br>1st | Pisces 12th<br>Aquarius 11th |
| Cancer<br>4th | | Capricorn<br>10th |
| Leo 5th<br>Virgo 6th | Libra<br>7th | Sagittarius 9th<br>Scorpio 8th |

*Houses for Aries Ascendant*

abdomen from the fifth house, and in the case of females, the womb, lap etc. Sixth house to Lumbar. From the seventh, two legs. Eighth to Gujhyasthan (Secret parts), anus. The Ninth House considers genitalia, testicles, penis, uterus, ovary etc. The tenth to thighs, eleventh to knees or adjacent region, and from the twelfth house, judge the feet. These houses are counted from the ascendant. For example, the first house of an Arise ascendant person is Arise. The second house is Taurus. The third is Gemini, and the fourth is Cancer, etc.

| | | |
|---|---|---|
| Taurus 11th<br>Gemini 12th | Aries 10th | Pisces 9th<br>Aquarius 8th |
| Cancer Ascendant 1st | | Capricorn 7th |
| Leo 2nd<br>Virgo 3rd | Libra 4th | Sagittarius 6th<br>Scorpio 5th |

*Houses for Cancer Ascendant*

The source of human diseases is mainly judged from the Sixth, eighth and twelfth places. First, it is to look after where these places' three lords or ruling planets are placed in any zodiac house. For example, if a person's sixth house lord is sitting in the second house, then we can understand the disease has captured his eyes, tongue, mouth, face, and/ or throat. Likewise, if the 6th, 8th or twelfth lords sit in the 5th, the person is suffering or may be suffering from some stomach problem because the fifth house denotes the belly, stomach, abdomen etc. But liver is ruled by the lord of 6th.

If any planet is weak or afflicted in any zodiac house, it can cause disease. For example, If Mars is placed in Aslesha Nakshatra in Cancer, it turns out to be weak in this house. Then the person can suffer from anaemia or may cause thalassemia. For example, if the Sun or the Moon is weak in the zodiac, the person may suffer from eye problems. (The Sun is the right eye, and the Moon is the left eye.)

Similarly, if any planet in any zodiac house situates weakly, then a particular part of the body may be affected by the disease of that planet. For example, if the malefic planets like Rahu, Ketu etc., are positioned in watery signs, then the worst type of boils, tumours etc., may occur. So even if Moon, Mars, Saturn, Rahu and Ketu are weak or malefic together in the zodiac, it can also identify the possibility of malignancy caused in the human body.

# Application of Music to Relieving Disease

So far, we have discussed the planetary influence on music, the taste in music, and the diagnosis of diseases etc., through astrology. This time we will talk about how to use music for the relief of those diseases or healing.

We have discussed in the previous chapter we cannot accept this fact arbitrarily that such a raga or tune can cure such and such disease. Therefore, why it cannot, how and which music can help in the treatment we shall briefly discuss in this chapter.

We know that music is a power of God, by which man can calm and control the mind in happiness, joy, grief, and sorrow. Not only that, the contribution of music in deity worship, motivation, performance, battlefield, leisure entertainment, and labour reduction are respectfully acknowledged. This power of God has been used for various purposes throughout the ages and achieved many satisfactory results. In the mantras of Rig Veda and Yajur Veda, the melody in the Sama Veda testify to the musical patterns. We have heard the story of playing music and the drum-like 'Kada-Nakada' instrument to increase the enthusiasm of soldiers of the war and the Great War. And in lifting big heavy stones, iron, etc., the labourers recite something rhythmic and use that rhythm to make their work easier. Decades ago, workers sang together and beat the roof while they built the house's roof. We see some of those instances even in this era.

Having gained experience from those examples, great doctors and musicologists have introduced music therapy in the medical field. 'Music therapy' means a method of treatment with the help of music. The triumph of music therapy in medical science is now almost everywhere. The treatment is also curing many incurable diseases through music therapy. From Alzheimer, Dementia, Arthritis, Stroke, Chronic pain, and Pregnancy problems to mental imbalance, psychosis, depressed mood, age-related depression, autism, laryngeal disorders and many other disorders are healed through music therapy. Nowadays, music therapy has become popular in our country also.

In America, rhythm, drums, beats, other musical instruments, methods, and melody are being discussed. Well-established research has revealed that lullaby has many benefits in developing the brain of children. In addition, music helps to control children's emotions, anger, sadness, shame, etc. We have heard that lately musicians are being hired abroad to sing to children. In short, human emotions, fatigue, enthusiasm, determination, and courage all can be controlled by music. This bunch of God's imperishable power is, on the one hand, the chanting of the yogi, the austerity of the ascetic, and on the other hand, the key to the patient's healing. From these examples, we can also consider using music as a medicine for disease relief and planetary peace.

## II

In this context, it is known that the cause of the actions of the world and human life is the act or influence of the planet. From human nature and character, his life, improvement, progress, suffering, and diseases, everything is the cause of the planet. Planetary causation is active everywhere in the living world, from plants to animals, insects, and humans.

The *Ishopanishad* said, "*Isha vasyamidam sarvam*"—everything in this world is created for the dwelling of God, or God covers everything in this world. We can say this in a slightly different way, "*Graha vasyamidam sarvam*"—everything in the world is covered by the influence of planets because the causality or effects of planets behind all events and actions is undeniable.

We have already discussed in the previous chapter that the planet governs each swar of music. Musicologists believe that the seven planets influence the seven swars of music. They observed the form and nature of the seven planets in the seven swars of music. Different emotions are expressed in people's minds by listening to songs or tunes because different *rasas* are released in the music by combining seven swars of music. The source of these *rasas* is a particular area of the brain. There, the *rasas* are released by the touch of the music, along with various chemical reactions. The source of these *rasas,* the release of chemicals, would never have been possible unless any planet was active in the melody of the music. Musicologists might have noticed the influence of the seven planets among the seven swars. Based on that formula, we would like to discuss how music can be used to cure the disease. For a long time, astrologers have suggested remedial measures such as gems, metals, roots, *yantrams,* etc., to save people from planetary disturbances. Now let's see if planetary adverseness can be prevented through music.

III

Musicologists and scholars have different opinions about the origin of the seven notes of music. They also have different views regarding the influence of the planets on the seven notes (swars) of music, which we have discussed earlier. So we will not appear into any new controversy about the origin of swars or the influence of planets over them.

We have already said that, according to traditional knowledge, the total number of musical swars is twelve. Seven are *Suddha* (natural), and five are *Bikrito* (flat & sharp). Sadaj, Rekhab, Gandhara, Madhyam, Pancham, Dhaivat, Nishad, i.e. Sa Re Ga Ma Pa Dha Ni are the seven *Suddha* swars. And *Komal* re, *Komal* ga, *Komal* dha, *Komal* ni and *Tibra* or *Kodi* MA are the five *Bikrito* swars. On the other hand, within the zodiac, the number of the signs is twelve; And the number of planets is twelve, namely the Sun, Moon, Mars, Mercury, Jupiter, Venus, Saturn, Rahu, Ketu, Uranus, Neptune and Pluto.

The number of Shuddha swar in music is seven. And the seven planets, Sun-Moon-Mars-Mercury-Jupiter-Venus and Saturn, predominate in the zodiac.

According to the musical scriptures, the influence of the seven planets Sun, Saturn, Mercury, Mars, Moon, Venus and Jupiter, respectively, exists in the seven swars like Sadaj, Rekhab, Gandhara, Madhyam, Pancham, Dhaibat and Nishad of music. And we have already discussed this in the previous chapter of this book that out of the twelve zodiac houses, apart from the Sun and the Moon, the other ten houses are fixed to the five planetary lords. Hence Sa and Pa are identified as the swars of the Sun and Moon, respectively. And accordingly, the Lords of the twelve houses of the zodiac are as follows –

| Sign | Lords | Vadi swar of music |
|---|---|---|
| Aries | Mars | Madhyam (Ma) |
| Taurus | Venus | Dhaivata (Dha) |
| Gemini | Mercury | Gandhara (Ga) |
| Cancer | Moon | Pancham (Pa) |
| Leo | Sun | Sadoj (Sa) |
| Vergo | Budha | Komal Gandhara (ga) |
| Libra | Sukra | Komal Dhaivata (dha) |
| Scorpio | Mars | Tibra Madhyam (MA) |
| Sagittarius | Jupiter | Nishad (Ni) |
| Capricorn | Saturn | Rekhab (Re) |
| Aquarius | Saturn | Komal Rekhab (Re) |
| Pisces | Jupiter | Komal Nishad (na) |

Based on this table, we will initially create a list of all the Ragas or tunes according to the predominance of *Vadi* and *Samvadi* Swars with the planets. Then according to the planet that caused the disease, the part of the body which is weak or diseased, that needs to make it strong and free from the illness, we suggest listening to those songs, which ragas are based on that planet-influenced swar. So the primary task is to prepare a list of planet-influenced ragas. In the ocean of Indian Music, the number of ragas is infinite. Therefore, in this brief discussion, it is impossible to write the names of all ragas. Thus, for any raga, we have to proceed according to the *Vadi* swar of a raga. A list is provided below to quickly understand which planet influences a particular raga or which planet governs the *Vadi* swar of a raga---

| *Ragas* | *Vadi swar* | *Planet* | *Samvadi* | *Planet* |
|---|---|---|---|---|
| Basant | Tar Sadoj (Sa') | Sun | Pancham (Pa) | Moon |
| Devgiri Bilawal | Sadoj (Sa) | Sun | Pancham (Pa) | Moon |
| Hansdhwani | Sadoj (Sa) | Sun | Pancham (Pa) | Moon |
| Mand | Sadoj (Sa) | Sun | Pancham (Pa) | Moon |
| Megh Malhar | Sadoj (Sa) | Sun | Pancham (Pa) | Moon |
| Nand | Sadoj (Sa) | Sun | Pancham (Pa) | Moon |
| Puriya Kalyan | Sadoj (Sa) | Sun | Pancham (Pa) | Moon |
| Tilak Kamod | Sadoj (Sa) | Sun | Pancham (Pa) | Moon |
| Basant Mukhari | Pancham (Pa) | Moon | Sadoj (Sa) | Sun |
| Bhankar | Pancham (Pa) | Moon | Sadoj (Sa ) | Sun |
| Chhayanat | Pancham (Pa) | Moon | Rekhab (Re) | Saturn |
| Debshree | Pancham (Pa) | Moon | Rekhab (Re) | Saturn |
| Desi | Pancham (Pa) | Moon | Sadoj (Sa) | Sun |
| Dhanashree | Pancham (Pa) | Moon | Sadoj (Sa) | Sun |
| Hanskinkini | Pancham (Pa) | Moon | Sadoj (Sa) | Sun |
| Kafi | Pancham (Pa) | Moon | Sadoj (Sa) | Sun |
| Kalavati | Pancham (Pa) | Moon | Sadoj (Sa) | Sun |
| Kalawati | Pancham (Pa) | Moon | Sadoj (Sa) | Sun |
| Kalingada | Pancham (Pa) | Moon | Sadoj (Sa) | Sun |
| Kamod | Pancham (Pa) | Moon | Rekhab (Re) | Saturn |
| Kirwani | Pancham (Pa) | Moon | Sadoj (Sa) | Sun |
| Madhukauns | Pancham (Pa) | Moon | Sadoj (Sa) | Sun |
| Madhuvanti | Pancham (Pa) | Moon | Sadoj (Sa) | Sun |
| Malhar | Pancham (Pa) | Moon | Sadoj (Sa) | Sun |
| Maru Bihag | Pancham (Pa) | Moon | Sadoj (Sa) | Sun |
| Multani | Pancham (Pa) | Moon | Sadoj (Sa) | Sun |
| Pahadi | Pancham (Pa) | Moon | Sadoj (Sa) | Sun |
| Patdeep | Pancham (Pa) | Moon | Sadoj (Sa) | Sun |
| Puriya Dhanashri | Pancham (Pa) | Moon | Sadoj (Sa) | Sun |

| *Raagas* | *Vadi swar* | *Planet* | *Samvadi* | *Planet* |
|---|---|---|---|---|
| Ramkeli | Pancham (Pa) | Moon | Sadoj (Sa) | Sun |
| Shivranjani | Pancham (Pa) | Moon | Sadoj (Sa) | Sun |
| Ahir Bhairav | Madhyam (Ma) | Mars | Sadoj (Sa) | Sun |
| Bageshri | Madhyam (Ma) | Mars | Sadoj (Sa) | Sun |
| Bahar | Madhyam (Ma) | Mars | Sadoj (Sa) | Sun |
| Bairagi | Madhyam (Ma) | Mars | Sadoj (Sa) | Sun |
| Bhairavi | Madhyam (Ma) | Mars | Sadoj (Sa) | Sun |
| Bhatiyar | Madhyam (Ma) | Mars | Sadoj (Sa) | Sun |
| Bhimpalasi | Madhyam (Ma) | Mars | Sadoj (Sa) | Sun |
| Chandrakauns | Madhyam (Ma) | Mars | Sadoj (Sa) | Sun |
| Charukeshi | Madhyam (Ma) | Mars | Sadoj (Sa) | Sun |
| Durga | Madhyam (Ma) | Mars | Sadoj (Sa) | Sun |
| Gaud Malhar | Madhyam (Ma) | Mars | Sadoj (Sa) | Sun |
| Gorakh Kalyan | Madhyam (Ma) | Mars | Sadoj (Sa) | Sun |
| Hemant | Madhyam (Ma) | Mars | Sadoj (Sa) | Sun |
| Jog | Madhyam (Ma) | Mars | Sadoj (Sa) | Sun |
| Jogiya | Madhyam (Ma) | Mars | Sadoj (Sa) | Sun |
| Kausi Kanada | Madhyam (Ma) | Mars | Sadoj (Sa) | Sun |
| Kedar | Madhyam (Ma) | Mars | Sadoj (Sa) | Sun |
| Lalit | Madhyam (Ma) | Mars | Sadoj (Sa) | Sun |
| Malgunji | Madhyam (Ma) | Mars | Sadoj (Sa) | Sun |
| Malkauns | Madhyam (Ma) | Mars | Sadoj (Sa) | Sun |
| Megh | Madhyam (Ma) | Mars | Sadoj (Sa) | Sun |
| Nat Bhairav | Madhyam (Ma) | Mars | Sadoj (Sa) | Sun |
| Nayaki Kanada | Madhyam (Ma) | Mars | Sadoj (Sa) | Sun |
| Bhoopali | Gandhar (Ga) | Mercury | Dhaibat (Dha) | Venus |
| Bihag | Gandhar (Ga) | Mercury | Nishad (Ni) | Jupiter |
| Bihagda | Gandhar (Ga) | Mercury | Nishad (Ni) | Jupiter |
| Dhani | Gandhar (Ga) | Mercury | Nishad (Ni) | Jupiter |
| Gaud Saarang | Gandhar (Ga) | Mercury | Dhaibat (Dha) | Venus |
| Jhinjhoti | Gandhar (Ga) | Mercury | Nishad (Ni) | Jupiter |
| Khamaj | Gandhar (Ga) | Mercury | Nishad (Ni) | Jupiter |
| Khambavati | Gandhar (Ga) | Mercury | Dhaibat (Dha) | Venus |
| Pilu | Gandhar (Ga) | Mercury | Nishad (Ni) | Jupiter |
| Poorvi | Gandhar (Ga) | Mercury | Nishad (Ni) | Jupiter |
| Puriya | Gandhar (Ga) | Mercury | Nishad (Ni) | Jupiter |
| Raageshri | Gandhar (Ga) | Mercury | Nishad (Ni) | Jupiter |
| Shankara | Gandhar (Ga) | Mercury | Nishad (Ni) | Jupiter |

| *Ragas* | *Vadi swar* | *Planet* | *Samvadi* | *Planet* |
|---|---|---|---|---|
| Shuddh Kalyan | Gandhar (Ga) | Mercury | Dhaibat (Dha) | Venus |
| Tilang | Gandhar (Ga) | Mercury | Nishad (Ni) | Jupiter |
| Yaman | Gandhar (Ga) | Mercury | Nishad (Ni) | Jupiter |
| Yaman Kalyan | Gandhar (Ga) | Mercury | Nishad (Ni) | Jupiter |
| Hemshree | Nishad (Ni) | Jupiter | Gandhar (Ga) | Mercury |
| Alhaiya Bilawal | Dhaibat (Dha) | Venus | Gandhar (Ga) | Mercury |
| Asavari | Komal Dha (dha) | Venus | Komal Ga (ga) | Mercury |
| Bhairav | Dhaibat (Dha) | Venus | Rekhab (Re) | Saturn |
| Bhoopal Todi | Dhaibat (Dha) | Venus | Gandhar (Ga) | Mercury |
| Bilaskhani Todi | Dhaibat (Dha) | Venus | Gandhar (Ga) | Mercury |
| Bilawal | Dhaibat (Dha) | Venus | Gandhar (Ga) | Mercury |
| Deshkar | Dhaibat (Dha) | Venus | Gandhar (Ga) | Mercury |
| Dev Gandhar | Dhaibat (Dha) | Venus | Gandhar (Ga) | Mercury |
| Gunkri | Dhaibat (Dha) | Venus | Rekhab (Re) | Saturn |
| Gurjari Todi | Dhaibat (Dha) | Venus | Rekhab (Re) | Saturn |
| Hamir | Dhaibat (Dha) | Venus | Gandhar (Ga) | Mercury |
| Hindol | Dhaibat (Dha) | Venus | Gandhar (Ga) | Mercury |
| Jaunpuri | Dhaibat (Dha) | Venus | Gandhar (Ga) | Mercury |
| Sohni | Dhaibat (Dha) | Venus | Gandhar (Ga) | Mercury |
| Todi | Dhaibat (Dha) | Venus | Gandhar (Ga) | Mercury |
| Vibhas | Dhaibat (Dha) | Venus | Rekhab (Re) | Saturn |
| Darbari | Rekhab (Re) | Saturn | Pancham (Pa) | Moon |
| Desh | Rekhab (Re) | Saturn | Pancham (Pa) | Moon |
| Jaijaiwanti | Rekhab (Re) | Saturn | Pancham (Pa) | Moon |
| Madhumad Sarang | Rekhab (Re) | Saturn | Pancham (Pa) | Moon |
| Marwa | Rekhab (Re) | Saturn | Dhaibat (Dha) | Venus |
| Sarang | Rekhab (Re) | Saturn | Pancham (Pa) | Moon |
| Sham Kalyan | Rekhab (Re) | Saturn | Pancham (Pa) | Moon |
| Shree | Rekhab (Re) | Saturn | Pancham (Pa) | Moon |
| Shuddh Sarang | Rekhab (Re) | Saturn | Pancham (Pa) | Moon |
| Vrindavani Sarang | Rekhab (Re) | Saturn | Pancham (Pa) | Moon |

## IV

Let's discuss how we could apply the ragas listed above for curing diseases.

Just as an astrologer recommends gemstones as a remedial measure after judging any person's horoscope; in this case, listening to music can be advised. For example, one whose Sun is weak or suffering from Sun-related problems could be asked to listen to those ragas or songs whose *Vadi* swar is Sadaj (Sa). Again, one who needs a treatment of Venus should listen to those songs whose *Vadi* swar is *Dhibat* (Dha) songs. According to astrological scriptures, as the remedies for malefic planets are advised, in the same way, listening to music should also be prescribed in this case.

Similarly, by reading the natal horoscope, judging which planet is the cause of the patient's disease, it should be suggested to play songs or ragas accordingly.

For example, suppose a Gemini ascendant suffers from lung problems or shortness of breath, as we know that the lung condition is understood from the fourth house of the ascendant. As per astrological scripture, one of the causes of shortness of breath is the position of the Trik (6th, 8th or 12th house) lord in the fourth house. Or, due to any reason, if the fourth house becomes weak the practitioner must stimulate the fourth house of that patient, i.e., Mercury, the lord of Virgo. So one should sing or listen to that raga whose Vadi swar is Ga (Gandhar), like Bhupali, Behag, Khambaj etc.

Similarly, a patient should listen to those songs or ragas whose *Vadi* swara is Pa (Pancham) to remove mental depression because Moon governs the mind and influences Pa. If Moon is aspected by Saturn, or the Moon is situated along with Saturn, or if Moon is weakened for some reason, mental problems like depression and unenthusiastic behavior may occur.

Again, if one has low blood pressure lack of confidence, the person should listen to those songs or ragas, whose *Vadi* swar is Ma (Madhyam). Because when Mars is weak, people have such problems. But if there is high pressure, then the swar of Mars (Ma) needs to be discarded. And the patient should listen to those songs in whose *Vadi* swar is influenced by Saturn.

For example, suppose a native has lost his self-confidence. Generally, astrology practitioners prescribe him the remedy of Mars; because Mars helps to increase self-confidence and self-esteem. In this case, we suggest the patient listen to those songs whose *Vadi* swar is influenced by Mars, like Bahar, Bageshri, Malkauns etc., as per the cited list, the astrologer can advise listening to which is necessary.

Again if the ascendant lord of Gemini (i.e., Mercury) is weak, then the person can listen to songs or tunes of Yaman, Bhupali, Bihag, or Khamaj raga to nourish his Mercury. Or one who wants to concentrate on meditation. Then the person should advise listening to songs whose Vadi swar is influenced by Jupiter or the 9th lord of that person's birth chart. The 9th lord brings the cause religious sense. And Jupiter's influenced swar is Nishad (Ni).

But in the ocean of Indian music, there are very few ragas whose *Vadi* swar is Nishad (Ni). So, in that case, the practitioner can advise that person to listen to those ragas whose *Samvadi* swar is Nishad (Ni), namely Raga Pilu, Shankara, Bihagda, Poorvi, Rageshri, Dhani etc.

If there is a malefic planet in one's birth horoscope, the swar influenced by that planet should be avoided as much as possible. For that reason, it should be looked after carefully that the raga or tune the patient is advised to listen to should not contain the song that increases that malefic planet. In this case, using those ragas or songs built by five swars (*Aurava*) or six swars (*Shadava*) may be suggested. At that same time, whether the particular malefic effector swar absent or weak in that raga also should be noted.

To avoid adverse swar, *Aurava* (five swars) or *Shadava* (six swars) class ragas or those where the particular swars are absent should be used. For example, as we know, Bhupali raga does not bear the Madhyam (Ma) nishad (Ni) swars. Now, if a person is very angry or moody, Bhupali raga can be sung if needed to calm him down because one of the factors of fierce anger or fierceness of temper is Mars.

As there is no Madhyam (Ma) in Bhupali raga, that Mars cannot gather any additional strength or support. Besides, the *Vadi* swar of Bhupali raga, being Gandhar (Ga), will be influenced by the person's Mercury, the planet that supports developing intelligence and judgement, and will help to increase his decision-making power and determination. Therefore a person whose mind is functioning well can never be mad with anger.

One of the causes of what neurologists call 'schizophrenia' is the mental aggravation caused by the conjunction or exchange of glance attitude of Rahu and Mars. So, in this case, along with other tunes, we can advise the patient to listen to raga Bhupal after examining the patient's horoscope.

V

Not only does it cure disease, but music therapy can also be used as a remedy for adverse planets. Astrologers suggest using pearls, emeralds, rubies, coral etc., to remedy the opposing planets. Likewise, listening to specific planet-influenced songs may be recommended instead of such planet gems.

The parents often worry that their children's studies are not going well. Then can suggest studying by listening to the melody of those songs, which are influenced by their study planets.

If children study while listening to music, it can reduce their monotony of study; also, the study planet (if it becomes weak) can gain strength or force by listening to music. Then, again, the healthy planet can get some more energy and enthusiasm if it may be playing those ragas, songs or tunes in the patient's house, whose Vadi swars are influenced by their study planets.

Also, remember that the person should advise not to listen to songs influenced by their malefic planet because the adversely affected tune can make the patient restless. If it is found that someone's mind is feeble, it is advisable not to let him listen to sad songs. Instead, we must suggest that he listen to lunar-influenced encouraging songs to invigorate his mind.

Remember one more thing in this context: just because you have to listen to music does not mean that you will play all-day loudly. It is improper to make another sick to cure one's disease. And it is not right to listen to music with headphones the entire day or for a long time. It can cause hearing problems. So it is recommended to listen to music in low or medium noise in the room. Moreover, it is better if the person can sing himself. Healing will be faster in that case by singing and listening.

As *Mooltrikona* (trine) is an essential factor in the zodiac, here, too, listening to the tune can be ordered based on the trine, that is, the planets located in the hundred twenty (120) degrees in the zodiac.

As we discussed earlier, on the selection of scale of music, here, we can think some thoughts about that too. Patients can sing according to the scale based on their *Mooltrikona* (trine). So even if they listen to music according to the scale, it can benefit them immensely.

The power of music is immeasurable. Music can do the impossible. It has been heard in the popular stories and legends of various famous musicians and their biography that music can kindle fire, bring rains as desire, untimely spring, stop mad elephants, and tame wild beasts like tigers.

May the medical system improve by utilising the enormous power of music, and may astrology and music therapy continue to benefit people. Furthermore, we hope music therapy will increase the practice widely and scientifically with more experiments.

# Determination of Dose for Music Therapy

Treating a patient must determine the measure of medicine required. The medication only functions correctly if the dosage is too high or too low. In the same way, in music therapy, it is not right to think that listening to a song for a long time throughout the day will cure the patient. Like that medicine, they should advise listening to particular music at particular times. If anyone wants to argue, we will say that that was an exception by showing the case of an unconscious patient of the SSKM hospital. In respect to our view, we will like to remember an example, just as a closed door can open by repeatedly knocking from outside but cannot rule out the possibility of breaking it.

However, we would like to say a few words about the dose of music therapy. We want to present here a formula by which astrologers can determine the dosage of music. Doctors have a definite rule for determining dosage, and so do astrologers. Depending on that, the astrologers indicate the quantity of any gem as a remedial measure. They advise people to keep corals, pearls, topaz, etc., for healing purposes. Because they have learned from scriptures like "*Jataka Parijat*" and "*Jataka Chandrika*" that they should arrange coral for Mars, pearls for

Moon, emeralds for Mercury, and topaz for Jupiter, and they prescribe different measures for use. Again by examining the horoscope, they can also know that all types of planets and gemstones cannot benefit everyone. The adverse effect of gems like pearl, coral, sapphire, topaz, etc., can harm some people. In that case, they consider and give them alternative advice as needed. As astrologers prescribe and advise the remedial measure of gems, we will now try to find the dose for music therapy based on that formula. In fact, no clue has been seen in music therapy on how to prescribe that dose.

A tune or rhythm needs to play to heal a person's illness, but it is necessary to think about how long that tune will play and how it can determine. Remember that anything, even music, can become boring if it plays for more than a specific period or length of time. Just as if a medicine gives more than the prescribed dose, it can harm the patient; similarly, the tune or rhythm can be detrimental if it plays for more than the measured time length. Therefore, during music therapy, it is necessary to advise the patient to listen to music for a specific length of time. Otherwise, the tune becomes monotonous and can embarrass the patient. Now we will devise a formula to determine the timeframe or doses of music here.

Generally, the specific size of the gemstone is calculated after considering the human body weight and the planet's strength. But in this case, we will give importance only to the planet's strength because a sick person's weight may lose or gain according to the extent of the patient's illness. So, we want to consider the body weight negligible in this case.

Here we want to remember one more thing. The disease first occurs in the patient's mind and then spreads to the body. The body creates immunity if the mind is all right or fit and thinking is healthy. Conditions take root in weak minds. So we calculate the measurement of medicine based on the planet's strength, excluding body weight. The planets' performance depends on their position in the zodiac. This performance is according to the stage of the planet. The planet has five stages based on the situated degree: child, boy, youth, adult, and old. Besides, the strength of each planet is determined by the zodiac. The scriptures mention ten strengths of the planet: Exaltation, Quadrangular, Directional, Diurnal, Lunar, Motional, Natural, and Positional Strength. Also, it should determine the power of the particular planet by considering the position of *Dagdhita* (burnt), *Kshobhita* (angry), *Udita* (rising), *Astomita* (setting), *Dipta* (bright), etc., and then should fix the measure of medicine. The healing or/and relief depends on this measurement. We want to use a simple formula to estimate or determine this dose.

We know that within thirty degrees, the planetary strength usually divides into five parts. Accordingly, each piece divides into 6 (six) degrees. If we look at the stage of the planet as a child, boy, youth, elderly, and old age, we will see that youth is the most decisive stage. In that ratio, the lower status is the boy and adult status. And the least powerful is the child and the old condition of the planet. This clause can write as-

(1) Young stage of the planet (the value of youth stage consider as 1).

(2) Boy and Elderly stage of the planet. (Consider the value of those statuses is 2).

(3) Child and Old hood of the planet. (considering the value of those stages is 3).

If thirty degrees divide into five parts, each part will be 6 (six) degrees. Therefore, we will treat these six (6) degrees as a unit.

According to this formula, the expected time required for listening to the tune at least twice a day (as *Ahoratra* divided into day and night) is–

2 (two) times x (30/5) x 1 (value of youth stage) = 12 minutes.

2 x (30/5) x 2 (value of boyhood or elderly hood stage) = 24 minutes in a day for boys or elderly hood.

2 (two) times x (30/5) x 3 (values of child or old hood stage) = 36 minutes for childhood and old hood.

According to the planet's strength, its duration can be 12 minutes, 24 minutes, or 36 minutes. If necessary, the period of those 24 or 36 minutes can be divided into two or three parts and listened to two or three times a day.

But it should be noticed that the patient listens only to the tune or rhythm while refraining from other activities. Because if the patient listens to music while doing some hand work or at the time reading some books or newspapers, they cannot adequately reach the effect of the melody on the mind. The patient should listen to music thoroughly and attentively at specific times as prescribed throughout the day.

# How to Treat with Music Therapy

The astrology practitioner and readers of this book also can treat music therapy by applying our just-invented process. It is an effortless process to cure or remit the pain of disease or to rescue a person from the adverseness of planets by following steps.

1. Make the patient's birth chart and examine it properly.
2. Find the disease of that patient from the birth chart.
3. Find the cause of the disease.
4. Find the patient's taste in music.
5. Select the scale of music if necessary.
6. Find the type of music and raga for the particular patient.
7. Calculate the dose of music.

Then advise the client to listen to the prescribed music or to sing the prescribed songs. And It is our belief that patients or clients can be cured of diseases after listening to or singing the prescribed songs..

# Appendix

List of ragas with Vadi and Samvadi swar and its planets sorted on Raga name, for quich scarch.

| *Ragas* | *Vadi swar* | *Planet* | *Samvadi* | *Planet* |
|---|---|---|---|---|
| Ahir Bhairav | Madhyam (Ma) | Mars | Sadoj (Sa) | Sun |
| Alhaiya Bilawal | Dhaibat (Dha) | Venus | Gandhar (Ga) | Mercury |
| Asavari | Komal Dha (dha) | Venus | Komal Ga (ga) | Mercury |
| Bageshri | Madhyam (Ma) | Mars | Sadoj (Sa) | Sun |
| Bahar | Madhyam (Ma) | Mars | Sadoj (Sa) | Sun |
| Bairagi | Madhyam (Ma) | Mars | Sadoj (Sa) | Sun |
| Basant Mukhari | Pancham (Pa) | Moon | Sadoj (Sa) | Sun |
| Basant | Tar Sadoj (Sa') | Sun | Pancham (Pa) | Moon |
| Bhairav | Dhaibat (Dha) | Venus | Rekhab (Re) | Saturn |
| Bhairavi | Madhyam (Ma) | Mars | Sadoj (Sa) | Sun |
| Bhankar | Pancham (Pa) | Moon | Sadoj (Sa ) | Sun |
| Bhatiyar | Madhyam (Ma) | Mars | Sadoj (Sa) | Sun |
| Bhimpalasi | Madhyam (Ma) | Mars | Sadoj (Sa) | Sun |
| Bhoopal Todi | Dhaibat (Dha) | Venus | Gandhar (Ga) | Mercury |
| Bhoopali | Gandhar (Ga) | Mercury | Dhaibat (Dha) | Venus |
| Bihag | Gandhar (Ga) | Mercury | Nishad (Ni) | Jupiter |
| Bihagda | Gandhar (Ga) | Mercury | Nishad (Ni) | Jupiter |
| Bilaskhani Todi | Dhaibat (Dha) | Venus | Gandhar (Ga) | Mercury |
| Bilawal | Dhaibat (Dha) | Venus | Gandhar (Ga) | Mercury |
| Chandrakauns | Madhyam (Ma) | Mars | Sadoj (Sa) | Sun |
| Charukeshi | Madhyam (Ma) | Mars | Sadoj (Sa) | Sun |
| Chhayanat | Pancham (Pa) | Moon | Rekhab (Re) | Saturn |
| Darbari | Rekhab (Re) | Saturn | Pancham (Pa) | Moon |
| Debshree | Pancham (Pa) | Moon | Rekhab (Re) | Saturn |
| Desh | Rekhab (Re) | Saturn | Pancham (Pa) | Moon |

| *Ragas* | *Vadi swar* | *Planet* | *Samvadi* | *Planet* |
|---|---|---|---|---|
| Deshkar | Dhaibat (Dha) | Venus | Gandhar (Ga) | Mercury |
| Desi | Pancham (Pa) | Moon | Sadoj (Sa) | Sun |
| Dev Gandhar | Dhaibat (Dha) | Venus | Gandhar (Ga) | Mercury |
| Devgiri Bilawal | Sadoj (Sa) | Sun | Pancham (Pa) | Moon |
| Dhanashree | Pancham (Pa) | Moon | Sadoj (Sa) | Sun |
| Dhani | Gandhar (Ga) | Mercury | Nishad (Ni) | Jupiter |
| Durga | Madhyam (Ma) | Mars | Sadoj (Sa) | Sun |
| Gaud Malhar | Madhyam (Ma) | Mars | Sadoj (Sa) | Sun |
| Gaud Saarang | Gandhar (Ga) | Mercury | Dhaibat (Dha) | Venus |
| Gorakh Kalyan | Madhyam (Ma) | Mars | Sadoj (Sa) | Sun |
| Gunkri | Dhaibat (Dha) | Venus | Rekhab (Re) | Saturn |
| Gurjari Todi | Dhaibat (Dha) | Venus | Rekhab (Re) | Saturn |
| Hamir | Dhaibat (Dha) | Venus | Gandhar (Ga) | Mercury |
| Hansdhwani | Sadoj (Sa) | Sun | Pancham (Pa) | Moon |
| Hanskinkini | Pancham (Pa) | Moon | Sadoj (Sa) | Sun |
| Hemant | Madhyam (Ma) | Mars | Sadoj (Sa) | Sun |
| Hemshree | Nishad (Ni) | Jupiter | Gandhar (Ga) | Mercury |
| Hindol | Dhaibat (Dha) | Venus | Gandhar (Ga) | Mercury |
| Jaijaiwanti | Rekhab (Re) | Saturn | Pancham (Pa) | Moon |
| Jaunpuri | Dhaibat (Dha) | Venus | Gandhar (Ga) | Mercury |
| Jhinjhoti | Gandhar (Ga) | Mercury | Nishad (Ni) | Jupiter |
| Jog | Madhyam (Ma) | Mars | Sadoj (Sa) | Sun |
| Jogiya | Madhyam (Ma) | Mars | Sadoj (Sa) | Sun |
| Kafi | Pancham (Pa) | Moon | Sadoj (Sa) | Sun |
| Kalavati | Pancham (Pa) | Moon | Sadoj (Sa) | Sun |
| Kalawati | Pancham (Pa) | Moon | Sadoj (Sa) | Sun |
| Kalingada | Pancham (Pa) | Moon | Sadoj (Sa) | Sun |
| Kamod | Pancham (Pa) | Moon | Rekhab (Re) | Saturn |
| Kausi Kanada | Madhyam (Ma) | Mars | Sadoj (Sa) | Sun |
| Kedar | Madhyam (Ma) | Mars | Sadoj (Sa) | Sun |
| Khamaj | Gandhar (Ga) | Mercury | Nishad (Ni) | Jupiter |
| Khambavati | Gandhar (Ga) | Mercury | Dhaibat (Dha) | Venus |
| Kirwani | Pancham (Pa) | Moon | Sadoj (Sa) | Sun |
| Lalit | Madhyam (Ma) | Mars | Sadoj (Sa) | Sun |
| Madhukauns | Pancham (Pa) | Moon | Sadoj (Sa) | Sun |
| Madhumad Sarang | Rekhab (Re) | Saturn | Pancham (Pa) | Moon |
| Madhuvanti | Pancham (Pa) | Moon | Sadoj (Sa) | Sun |
| Malgunji | Madhyam (Ma) | Mars | Sadoj (Sa) | Sun |

| *Ragas* | *Vadi swar* | *Planet* | *Samvadi* | *Planet* |
|---|---|---|---|---|
| Malhar | Pancham (Pa) | Moon | Sadoj (Sa) | Sun |
| Malkauns | Madhyam (Ma) | Mars | Sadoj (Sa) | Sun |
| Mand | Sadoj (Sa) | Sun | Pancham (Pa) | Moon |
| Maru Bihag | Pancham (Pa) | Moon | Sadoj (Sa) | Sun |
| Marwa | Rekhab (Re) | Saturn | Dhaibat (Dha) | Venus |
| Megh Malhar | Sadoj (Sa) | Sun | Pancham (Pa) | Moon |
| Megh | Madhyam (Ma) | Mars | Sadoj (Sa) | Sun |
| Multani | Pancham (Pa) | Moon | Sadoj (Sa) | Sun |
| Nand | Sadoj (Sa) | Sun | Pancham (Pa) | Moon |
| Nat Bhairav | Madhyam (Ma) | Mars | Sadoj (Sa) | Sun |
| Nayaki Kanada | Madhyam (Ma) | Mars | Sadoj (Sa) | Sun |
| Pahadi | Pancham (Pa) | Moon | Sadoj (Sa) | Sun |
| Patdeep | Pancham (Pa) | Moon | Sadoj (Sa) | Sun |
| Pilu | Gandhar (Ga) | Mercury | Nishad (Ni) | Jupiter |
| Poorvi | Gandhar (Ga) | Mercury | Nishad (Ni) | Jupiter |
| Puriya Dhanashri | Pancham (Pa) | Moon | Sadoj (Sa) | Sun |
| Puriya Kalyan | Sadoj (Sa) | Sun | Pancham (Pa) | Moon |
| Puriya | Gandhar (Ga) | Mercury | Nishad (Ni) | Jupiter |
| Raageshri | Gandhar (Ga) | Mercury | Nishad (Ni) | Jupiter |
| Ramkeli | Pancham (Pa) | Moon | Sadoj (Sa) | Sun |
| Sarang | Rekhab (Re) | Saturn | Pancham (Pa) | Moon |
| Sham Kalyan | Rekhab (Re) | Saturn | Pancham (Pa) | Moon |
| Shankara | Gandhar (Ga) | Mercury | Nishad (Ni) | Jupiter |
| Shivranjani | Pancham (Pa) | Moon | Sadoj (Sa) | Sun |
| Shree | Rekhab (Re) | Saturn | Pancham (Pa) | Moon |
| Shuddh Kalyan | Gandhar (Ga) | Mercury | Dhaibat (Dha) | Venus |
| Shuddh Sarang | Rekhab (Re) | Saturn | Pancham (Pa) | Moon |
| Sohni | Dhaibat (Dha) | Venus | Gandhar (Ga) | Mercury |
| Tilak Kamod | Sadoj (Sa) | Sun | Pancham (Pa) | Moon |
| Tilang | Gandhar (Ga) | Mercury | Nishad (Ni) | Jupiter |
| Todi | Dhaibat (Dha) | Venus | Gandhar (Ga) | Mercury |
| Vibhas | Dhaibat (Dha) | Venus | Rekhab (Re) | Saturn |
| Vrindavani Sarang | Rekhab (Re) | Saturn | Pancham (Pa) | Moon |
| Yaman Kalyan | Gandhar (Ga) | Mercury | Nishad (Ni) | Jupiter |
| Yaman | Gandhar (Ga) | Mercury | Nishad (Ni) | Jupiter |

# Bibliography

Alan Leo's Dictionary of Astrology - Vivian E. Robson; Sagar Publication; 1973.

An Introduction to Astrology - William Lilly; London, July 1834.

Astrology X-Rayed (The Wisdom of Heavens) Exoteric and Esoteric - Sukracharya; Auther self, January 1990.

Bharate Jyotishcharcha O Kosti-bicharer Sutraboli - by Sri Narendranath Bagal.

Chandeshwar - Collected by Sri Rasikmohon Chattopadhyay, publish by author self.

Chandronmilan - Sri Rashikmohon Chattopadhyay, Published by author self.

Chelebelar Dinguli - Punyalata Chakraborty, New Script, Ashwin 1365 [Sep-Oct 1958]

Dictionary of Astrology - Jyotirvid J.N. Bhasin; Ranjan Publication, New Delhi; 2014.

Encyclopedia of Astrology - Nicholas de Vore, The Philosophical Library, June 1947.

Geetsutrasar - Krishnadhan bandyapadhyay, Edited by Niharbindu Chowdhury, A. Mukherjee & Co. Pvt. Ltd, Pous 1362 (January 1956).

Indian Astrology, Sex, Marriage & Children - Parimal Purkayastha; ?; 1956.

Jaiminiya Upadesh Sutram - Pandit Ramgopal Ray Compiled by Jyotirbinod Tantrabhushan, Publisher Sri Gourab Ray, 1387.

Jatak Ballabh - Pandit Sri Radhaballabh smriti byakaran jyotisthirtha, Publish by the author self, 1860 Shakabda.

Jatak Parijat - by Sri Daibagnyo Baidyanath, Pandit Kapileshear Shastri & Pandit Srimatriprasad Shastri, Choukhamba Sanskrit Sansthan, Baranasi, 2036 Sambat.

Jyotirbignan Kalpalatika - ? (Title page is missing)

Jyotish Obhidhan - Basumitra Majumder, Joydurga Library, 15 April 2021.

Jyotish Digdarshan - Sukracharya, The Calcutta Astrological Society, 25 Dec 1997.

Jyotish Kalpadrum - by Rasikmohan Chattapadhyay (Title page is missing)

Jyotisher Aloke Sangeet Chikitsa - Basumitra Majumder, Articles are published in verious Astrological Megazine. Since - 1997 to 2022.

K.P. Navaratnamala - Shri Tin Win, Compiled by Kanak Bosmia.Music Therapy and Ayurveda - by Dr. Yashashri Arun Vitonde, Notion Press, 6th January 2021.

Marifun Nagmat - Raja Nawab Ali, Sangeet Karjalaya, Hatras, 3rd. ed. 1974.

Music Therapy - Collected and Edited by Ishita Mukhopadhyay, Best Books, January 2020.

Naradiya Shiskah - Didhiti Biswas, Papyras, June 2000.

Raag O Rup (Both Part) - Swami Prajnanananda, Sriramkrishna Vedanta Math, 1961 & 1982.

Sangeet Chikitsa - Dr. J. Pal M.I.M Samvedi, Dr. J. Pal Chamberlane Road, Lahore. 1938.

Sangeet Damadar - Sri Subhankar, Edited by Gourinath Shastri & Gobindagopal Mukhopadhyay, Sanskrit College, Kolkata, 1960.

Sangeet Ratnakar - Edited by Dr. Pradip Kumar Ghosh, Paschimbanga Rajya Sangeet Academi, 1994.

Swar-Mel-Kalanidhi - Ramamatya, Edited by Dr. Pradip Kumar Ghosh, Research Institute of Musicology, Kolkata. January 1991.

The miracle of Music Therapy by Rajendar Menon, Pustak Mahal, Edition 2012.

The Astrologers and their Creed (An Historical Outline) - Christopher McIntosh; Frederick A. Praeger, New York; 1969.

A Sanskrit-English Dictionary - Sir Monier Monier-Williams; Motilal Banarsidass; 1986.

Compact Oxford Dictionary & Thesaurus - Edited by Catherine Soanes and Sara Hawker; Oxford University Press; 2008.

Printed by Libri Plureos GmbH in Hamburg, Germany